The Pacific Northwest

by Raymond A. Wohlrabe

THE PACIFIC NORTHWEST

EXPLORING SOLAR ENERGY

EXPLORING ELECTROSTATICS

The Pacific Northwest

QUEEN
CHARLOTTE
ISLANDS

Prince Rupert

Kitimat

Ocean Falls

0   50   100   150   200

Miles

PACIFIC OCEAN

QUEEN CHARLOTTE ST.

VANCOUVER ISLAND

STRAIT OF GEORGIA

STRAIT OF
JUAN DE FUCA

BRITISH COLUMBIA

COAST MOUNTAIN RANGE

FRASER R.

FRASER R.

THOMPSON R.

Kamloops

Nanaimo

Vancouver
New Westminster

Victoria

MT. SHUKSAN
MT. BAKER
Bellingham

OLYMPIC
NAT. PK.

Port Townsend

Bremerton

Everett
Seattle

PUGET SOUND

Tacoma

Olympia

MT.
RAINIER

WENATCHEE MT.

MT.
ADAMS

McBride
Barkerville

R. ATHABASCA R.

ROCKY MTS.

MONASHEE MTS.

COLUMBIA R.

GLACIER
NAT. PK.

Banff

Vernon

Kelowna
Penticton

OKANOGAN R.

Trail

ROOSEVELT L.

Grand
Coulee

SPOKANE R.

Spokane

Coeur D'Alene

Wallace

COLUMBIA R.

WASHINGTON

CASCADE RANGE

Astoria

Tillamook

Vancouver

Portland

Oregon City

Salem

Newport

Eugene

Reedsport

Coos Bay

WILLAMETTE R.

Hood River

Kennewick

The Dalles

MT. HOOD

MT. JEFFERSON

Pasco

Walla Walla

RIVER

Pendleton

BLUE MTS.

COLUMBIA RIVER

SNAKE R.

SNAKE
CANYON R.

SALMON R.

BITTERROOT RANGE

IDAHO

OREGON

Bend

CRATER L.

KLAMATH R.

Klamath
Falls

CASCADE RANGE

Boise

SNAKE R.

Ketchum

CRATERS OF THE
MOON NAT. MON.

Idaho Falls

Twin
Falls

Pocatello

Ascher!

N
W   E
S

PACIFIC OCEAN

The
Pacific Northwest

RAYMOND A. WOHLRABE

THE WORLD PUBLISHING COMPANY
CLEVELAND AND NEW YORK

The author and The World Publishing Company wish to thank the following for permission to reproduce their photographs in this book:

Alcan Aluminum, Ltd., p. 108; Boeing Company, p. 95; British Columbia Government, p. 11; Canadian Government Travel Bureau, pp. 91, 101; Department of Fisheries of Canada, pp. 87, 88; Idaho State Department of Commerce and Development, p. 71, pp. 82–83; Nebraska State Historical Society, p. 35; Ocean Spray Cranberries, Inc., p. 41; Oregon Historical Society, p. 29; Oregon State Highway Department, pp. 14, 64, 69, 99, 107, 116; Spokane Chamber of Commerce, p. 60; Sun Valley News Bureau, pp. 75, 119; Tacoma Chamber of Commerce, Winfield Brown Photo, p. 43; Washington State Department of Commerce and Economic Development, pp. 13, 45, 52, 54, 59, 114, and the jacket photograph showing Thornton Lake, Washington; Washington State Department of Commerce and Economic Development, Cowley Photo, back of the jacket showing Olympia, Washington; Washington State Game Department, p. 112; Washington State Historical Society, p. 26; Weyerhaeuser Company, pp. 104, 105.

Published by The World Publishing Company
2231 West 110th Street, Cleveland, Ohio 44102
Published simultaneously in Canada by
Nelson, Foster & Scott Ltd.
Library of Congress catalog card number: 68-14695
Copyright © 1968 by Raymond A. Wohlrabe
Designed by Jack Jaget

Contents

Many thanks go to those individuals whose suggestions and help have been most sincerely appreciated. They include those who so generously cooperated by providing many of the photographs used as illustrations. Members of the staffs of various state and provincial departments, historical societies, and the public relations departments of companies engaged in Pacific Northwest industry have generously given of their time to provide needed information. Thanks go to Mrs. Joan Delaney, Photo Librarian of the Washington State Department of Commerce and Economic Development. To Mrs. Joan Knight of The World Publishing Company I am especially grateful for her help in suggesting changes and additions in the manuscript.

—RAYMOND A. WOHLRABE
Seattle, Washington.

A Multimillion-Year
Landscaping Project

THE PACIFIC NORTHWEST is a region of rugged green seacoast, forested mountains, and, in its eastern half, a broad dry plateau. It reaches from central British Columbia to the California state line; from the Pacific Ocean across mountain ranges, plateaus, and deserts to the foothills of the Rockies. The states of Idaho, Oregon, and Washington, and the lower part of the Canadian province of British Columbia are included.

Except in the great basin and the deserts of the eastern half, the Pacific Northwest abounds in magnificent mountain ranges. The Cascade Range has high peaks snow-capped all year, some with complex glacier systems, and is the backbone of the region. Beyond the Canadian border are British Columbia's Coast Mountains flanked on the east by the Cariboo, Columbia, and Cascade ranges. West of the Cascades in Washington the Olympics form a rampart of snowy peaks between the Pacific Ocean and Puget Sound, the long inland extension of the sea with three hundred islands and two thousand miles of shoreline. The Coast Range lies between the sea and the Cascades in western Oregon. The Blue Mountains in Oregon's cattle country lie between the Cascades and the Rockies. Most of the Idaho panhandle is covered by the Clearwater and Salmon River mountains and her eastern boundary with Montana follows the crest of the Bitterroot Range.

About sixty million years ago nature started the colossal task of shaping the Pacific Northwest as we know it today. At that time ocean waves rolled across the region. They lapped against a high promontory

9

jutting westward from highlands far to the east where the Blue Mountains are now. Powerful forces exerting constant pressure under the ocean floor eventually pushed up a long mountainous ridge that reached from California to Alaska. Then volcanic activity cracked the earth's surface. Molten lava was released. The ridge became a chain of low mountains. This was the beginning of the Cascade Range. This ridge formed a barrier between the ocean to the west and an inland sea to the east.

The floor of the inland sea sank for a period of time before it began to rise again. Pent-up waters sought an outlet. The lowest and weakest part of the Cascade Range became the spillway. Water that poured through carved a deep trough that eventually became the eighty-mile Columbia River gorge with its rapids, cascades, and waterfalls. Far to the west of the Cascades in what is Oregon today, a chain of small volcanic islands appeared above the surface of the ocean and spumed fiery lava and clouds of dust. Slowly, over many millenia, they joined to become a sea dike, the low Coast Range, that eventually stretched from big Siskiyou Island to southeastern Alaska. The southern part of the trough between it and the Cascades became the Willamette valley; the northern part, Puget Sound and the Cowlitz plain.

Even more spectacular were the changes that took place during the millions of years that still remained before the dawn of history. To piece together the dramatic story, geologists used clues they found embedded in rock formations. They examined samplings of sediment that had settled long ago. Boulders strewn across a plain; marks left where waves had dashed against barren uplifts; and the etchings of skeletons, leaves, and stems on rock fractured from deposits of shale all had meaning. Anthropologists sifted the dust and debris from cavern floors. They studied arrowheads, crude tools, and articles woven of the fibers from roots and stems.

Fossil skeletons have been found in the high plateau in what is now eastern Washington and the Oregon Desert. This region, in early geological periods, was dotted with lakes and jungles of tropical vegetation. There is ample proof that sheeplike three-toed horses, prehistoric camels, and saber-toothed cats lived here until lava flows drove them into adjacent regions or destroyed them. A sea of lava plugged drainage routes and led to the formation of large lakes. During this time some of the peaks of the Cascade Range attained heights of two or three miles above sea level. This era of prehistory ended with the dawn of the ice age which, broken by several short periods of rising temperatures, lasted for a million years.

Glaciers such as this one west of Mount Hickman in British Columbia continue to shape the Pacific Northwest today.

Nature used the million-year winter to polish what had been done and carve new features. An ice sheet or glacier covered British Columbia and tongues of ice nearly a thousand feet thick reached into the Columbia plateau. The peaks of the highest mountains poked above its surface. It spread over northern Idaho and western Montana. One of its lobes blocked the channel of the Columbia River near where the Grand Coulee Dam is today and forced the river to turn south. Other tongues of ice blocked the Spokane River valley. A glacier's enormous weight depresses the part of the earth's crust it covers. Rock layers are ground down as the glacier moves. Thus, huge rivers of glacial ice did a massive bulldozing job as they scooped out the basins for the Chelan, Pend Oreille, and Coeur d'Alene lakes. The ice sheet blocked rivers flowing from western Montana, forming a gigantic dike that created a lake two thousand feet deep—Lake Missoula in Montana.

Rising temperatures brought the ice age to an end about fifteen thousand years ago and led to some of the most dramatic changes in nature's landscaping project. The glaciers began to melt, releasing huge volumes of water which raced across the area bounded by the Columbia, Spokane, and Snake rivers. Icebergs broken from the glaciers floated onto the Columbia plateau and dropped boulders and gravel as they melted. Meltwater filled ice and boulder-choked river channels and sent water flooding across their banks. New channels were cut so deeply in the surface of the land by the rushing waters that the bedrock of lava laid down millions of years before was uncovered. Large islands were created as the water carved its way into the earth's thick deposit of sand and dust, and wide gulches or coulees were formed by the floods. This Columbia plateau region is known to geologists today as the "channeled scablands." The Grand Coulee, as we call the channel formed by the detour of the Columbia River, begins just south of the Grand Coulee Dam. It is one of the huge gulches that cuts through the surface of the Columbia plateau. The Grand Coulee averages three miles across and in places its floor is a thousand feet below the surrounding country.

Many waterfalls appeared at this time. At one point in its course the Columbia River plunged nine hundred feet from a basaltic ledge to create a waterfall that was five miles wide. This is believed to have been the largest waterfall the world has ever seen. Another prehistoric waterfall was almost as large. Enough of what can be called its skeleton remains to help us picture what it was like. This is known as the Dry Falls of central Washington. We can see that its waters plunged more than four hundred feet to the potholes it carved out of the coulee floor. This cataract was more than twice as high as Niagara Falls and the volume of water flowing over its brink was eighty times as great. When the glaciers began to melt, and the prehistoric flood began, the falls were originally farther south. The rushing water broke away the rock of the precipice over which it plunged and the falls retreated upstream. This accounts for the chain of lakes now in the potholes some distance below Dry Falls called the Sun Lakes.

Volcanic forces went to work again when the ice age was over. Mount Rainier, in the Cascades, blew its top. It once had an altitude of about 16,000 feet; however, as a result of this violent eruption two thousand feet were lost and a wide crater was formed. The heat from this crater melts the snow that falls in it and produces steam. The crater can be seen only from the air. Most of the peak is covered with snow all year round. Proof of other volcanic activity is abundant in the Pacific Northwest. In prehistoric times Mount Mazama spumed molten lava during frequent eruptions. Lava also flowed through subterranean passageways from the cauldron of its interior. During an eruption ten thousand years ago the top of Mount Mazama collapsed and left a yawning crater. As volcanic action died a few cinder cones formed in the pit. Over the centuries water from rain and snow formed a lake about a third of a mile deep in the crater. The largest of the cinder cones pokes above the lake's surface and is known as Wizard Island. Crater Lake, as it is called, is the most beautiful lake in southern Oregon. Most of the long rays of light which penetrate its surface are absorbed and only the short blue rays are reflected, giving it its brilliant blue color.

Several dormant and extinct volcanoes, their slopes covered by glaciers and their summits crowned with snow fields, lie above the timberline along the crest of the Cascade Range. The highest is Mount Rainier, its summit at 14,410 feet. Mount Baker (10,750 ft.), near Bellingham in northern Washington, Mount Adams (12,307 ft.), and Mount St. Helens (9,671 ft.) are other prominent peaks on the skyline of western Washington. Hikers who use the well-marked Cascade Crest Trail have superb views of these snow-covered sentinels. Mount Olympus (8,150

The Dry Falls in central Washington. This is all that remains of a prehistoric waterfall that was more than twice as high as Niagara Falls.

ft.) is in the Olympic Range on the peninsula between the Pacific Ocean and Puget Sound. Mount Hood (11,245 ft.) is the highest in Oregon. Near its base is the winter sports area centered at Timberline Lodge. Three snow-capped peaks in southern Oregon, the Three Sisters, were formed along the rim of the crater left after an eruption of the huge prehistoric peak geologists call Mount Multnomah.

Nature created a chain of islands off the British Columbia mainland by permitting a low mountain range to sink until all but its peaks were submerged. She continues her work. Perhaps millions of years from now the landscape of the Pacific Northwest will be quite different. For us today she has created a region of great natural beauty with magnificent peaks, rugged coastlines, deserts, and rolling hills.

Crater Lake, one of the most beautiful lakes in Oregon, is set in the crater of the extinct volcano, Mount Mazama. Wizard Island pokes above the surface of the lake's brilliant blue waters.

Indians, Totem Poles, and Potlatches

L ONG BEFORE the white man came to the Pacific Northwest, Indians seeking better hunting and fishing grounds had settled the land. Their ancestors had struggled across the steppes of Siberia to the Pacific coast of Asia about fifteen thousand years ago. They had stumbled through fog and were buffeted by winds out of the Arctic as they made their way over the prehistoric land bridge which once linked Asia with Alaska. Over the centuries their descendants worked southward into the continent and down to the Pacific coast.

By the time the first explorers came to the Pacific Northwest in the eighteenth century, it is believed that about one hundred and eighty thousand Indians lived in the entire region. There were some one hundred and twenty "tribes" by the seventeenth century, although the term "tribe" should not really be used to describe the many bands of Indians living in the region who had little or no tribal organization. It is more accurate to divide the Indians into three large groups—the canoe, plateau, and basin peoples.

Nature set the pattern of life for the Indians of the northwest long before the great "winged canoes" of the explorers dropped anchor there. Each June she carpeted the poorly drained meadows of the plateau country with blue camas blossoms. When the plants withered and dried under the midsummer sun, Indians gathered the bulbs for winter food. The plateau people came from their villages with digging sticks to the southern slopes of hills for their share of the juicy roots from the first plants to respond to the warmth of spring. Nature melted the snowpack

15

in the mountains. Floodwaters flowed into the valleys. The first horde of silver salmon began migrating to the headwaters of the rivers to spawn. This was the signal for bands of Indians to travel to fishing stations with spears and nets. Oil-rich salmon, smoked or dried, was a major food. Where the waters of the Columbia churned across ridges of basalt near what is now the city of The Dalles was a favorite fishing spot of the Chinooks. Men and boys spent long hours with spears and nets on makeshift platforms below the falls and above the rapids. The women cleaned the catch in preparation for drying and smoking it. When camp was broken their harvest of fish for the winter was taken to their villages by canoe. Nature stocked the forests with deer, elk, bear, and mountain goats. She provided berries to be picked, pressed into cakes, and dried.

Abundance of food was the yardstick by which the wealth of an Indian was gauged. The canoe people on the coast were rated wealthy. Most of the plateau Indians fared quite well although there were some lean years and periods of near starvation. Only the people of the great basin south of the big bend of the Columbia and the Snake could be considered truly poor.

The area between the Pacific Ocean and the Cascades where the canoe people lived was a land of plenty with a mild climate. It had dense forests of Douglas fir, red or yellow cedar, hemlock, and spruce. Logs from these trees were easily split with a stone adze and a wooden wedge. These logs provided the planks and poles for their houses. Plank-house villages, as they are known, stood on riverbanks or the shores of well-protected coves along the coast. The most elaborate of these villages were located along the beaches of the British Columbia mainland, Vancouver Island, and the Queen Charlotte Islands. Each house was rectangular, and measured thirty by fifty or more feet. A central fire served the needs of all of the occupants, who were many since several families usually lived in one house. Smoke was let out through a hole in the roof. Much of the canoe people's clothing was woven of fibers from cedar bark. During the rainy season cone-shaped hats and rain capes of cedar bark were worn. Food was abundant. Salmon and halibut were supplemented by clams, crabs, and other shellfish gathered at the village doorstep at ebb tide.

Dugouts or canoes made from cedar logs were the only means of transportation. The largest dugouts, fashioned from logs more than fifty feet long, were for whaling, hunting seals and sea otters, raids on tribes down the coast, and ceremonial rites. The smaller-size dugouts were used for fishing, visiting neighbors, and exploring.

Dugout canoes such as this one were used by the Indians who lived near the mouth of the Columbia River.

The techniques for building a dugout were well developed by the canoe people, especially among the Haida of the north coast. A log was hollowed out with an adze or was carefully burned out. Then it was filled with water heated to boiling with hot stones. This softened the wood of the walls so that they could be stretched outward by propping poles of various lengths between them. After the main body was finished a prow and a stern of wood ornamented with carved symbolic figures were firmly attached with ropes of cedar fiber.

The canoe Indians of the British Columbia coast and southeastern Alaska had a flare for art. They expressed it by carving animal figures and faces in wood. Their abundance of food and materials for shelters left them plenty of time for other activities. There was ample leisure for wood-sculpturing, weaving baskets of spruce and cedar fibers, telling tall tales and boasting. Totem poles, ceremonial masks carved from wood, wooden boxes and dishes ornamented with carved symbols, and other well-designed objects were the products these leisure hours made possible.

Memorial totem poles were erected in front of many of the houses of a village. Animal and human forms and mythical monsters carefully carved in the wood revealed noteworthy incidents in the life of a person or his ancestors. Some totem poles served as house posts. An elaborate central house post, tall and beautifully carved, was quite common. The animal form at its base had a mouth large enough to serve as a door or entrance to the house. Mortuary poles erected beside a grave or supporting a grave box which held the remains of the deceased were appropriately designed and carved.

Preparing a totem pole required much planning and the skill of a good totem carver. A tall tree was selected and felled. Decisions about the animal figures to be included were made after lengthy discussions. Much of the sculpturing was done with an adze and then the surface was polished with abrasive materials like the skin of a dogfish or scouring rushes gathered from neighboring salt marshes. The symbolic animal figures are easily recognized. Certain prominent characteristics are emphasized in each. The sharp teeth and flat tail with distinctive crosshatching identifies the beaver. Claws, paws, and large teeth are features of the bear. The raven with widespread wings and a long straight beak was a family crest frequently used. A heavy beak curved sharply downward at the tip was a feature of the eagle. There were also figures of the mythical thunderbird, the killer whale, the shark, the frog, and other animals. Totem-pole carvers are not as common today as they were in the last century. However, some Indian villages with poles either standing or leaning in various stages of decay can still be found. One is Cape Mudge, a village on an island in the Strait of Georgia only a few minutes by ferry from the town of Campbell River on Vancouver Island. Such villages are more plentiful in the Queen Charlotte Islands and the Hazelton area inland between the Coast and Omineca mountains on the Prince George-Prince Rupert highway.

The potlatch was another custom belonging to many of the tribes of canoe people. This was a festival featuring speeches, feasting, dances by participants wearing carved wooden masks, and, most important, the giving away of the host's accumulated wealth as gifts to the guests. Preparations could require several months or longer. A potlatch was an occasion for a great display of wealth by the host and the nobles of his village. Elaborate ceremonial robes of bearskin or sea-otter fur and blankets woven of mountain-goat hair were worn. A marriage, the inheritance of the office of chief, the event of a chief's child catching his first fish or any other of many reasons could warrant a potlatch. The underlying motive was, of course, to contribute to the prestige of the host; the gift-giving was definitely meant to do this. But besides enhancing the prestige of the host, the potlatch was designed to increase his wealth. Articles of great value like carved chests, blankets, and robes

Totem poles were elaborate and beautifully carved.

were passed on to the guests. The host knew that he in turn would be invited to potlatches given by each of his guests and that they would attempt to outdo him in lavish generosity.

Life was not as easy or colorful for many of the bands of plateau people east of the Cascades. They were seminomadic, moving about in search of food, but always returning to their winter villages. They traveled on foot. If their village, which was usually small, bordered a lake or stream, they would use dugouts. However, their dugouts were much less elaborate than those of their neighbors across the mountains to the west.

The home of the plateau Indian was a very simple shelter, especially if he lived in the dry treeless sagebrush country of central Washington. A wide pit was dug and then covered with a cone-shaped roof of poles and willow-fiber mats. Atop this was a covering of sod, clay, and brush. Access to the house was by way of the smoke hole at the tip of the cone and by ladder to the floor of the pit. A temporary summer shelter at fishing stations and gathering grounds was made of mats and poles.

Tribal organization was almost nonexistent among the Sanpoil, Nespelem, and Okanogan tribes living in the central and northern part of the plateau. They were members of the Salish language-speaking group. The Sanpoils were a peace-loving people who never fought other tribes or quarreled with each other. When attacked by warlike neighbors they offered no defense. Theirs was a group in which all men were considered equal, even to sharing the food they gathered. Unlike the canoe Indians of the coast, they had no slaves and no class distinctions.

Introduction of the horse to the plateau and basin people greatly changed their way of life. The Bannock and Paiute Indians who later became known quite generally as the Shoshonis or Snakes had horses late in the seventeenth century. They got them from Indians of the southwest who had obtained them from the Spaniards. The Nez Percé, a warlike people who lived on the eastern edge of the plateau, enthusiastically accepted the horse. It made it possible for them to travel far from home on buffalo hunts or on raids to obtain slaves which they usually traded for horses. They began breeding horses and letting them graze on the rich grasslands of the plateau. The Appaloosa was their favorite—a two-toned, polka-dotted animal with plenty of spirit and endurance. A Nez Percé warrior astride his Appaloosa and wearing the eagle-feather headdress he had adopted from other tribes was indeed an imposing figure!

South of the Bitterroot Range and the Salmon River Mountains in Idaho and the Blue Mountains of Oregon lies the semidesert region of the Great Basin. This is largely a treeless land dotted with a few mountain ranges. Here the poorest Indians of the Pacific Northwest—the basin people—used to live. For their food they dug up roots with digging sticks, and ate seeds of plants, acorns, and insects and larvae. At times they were able to supplement this meager diet with antelope, deer, or rabbit. Their shelters were crude hovels of dirt and brush. Mats, cooking baskets, and what little clothing they wore were made of the fibers of plants found in the tule marshes of the region. The Bannocks and northern Paiutes belonged to this group.

Today much of the old way of life of the Indian is merely a memory. Many of his legends are forgotten. The descendants of the Haida have forgotten about dugouts, and now own gas boats that join the herring fleet off Canada's west coast. Very few Indians today know how to carve a totem pole or a ceremonial mask. Basket-weaving is another craft which has all but disappeared. Attempts are being made, however, to train the present generation in the skills that made the artistic creations of their forefathers so distinctive.

Explorers, Traders, and Missionaries

IN THE SPRING of 1579 red-bearded Sir Francis Drake, the English buccaneer, sailed his one-hundred-ton ship, the *Golden Hind,* within sight of Cape Blanco on the southern Oregon coast. On his way there he had plundered Spanish towns along the west coast of the Americas and relieved a Manila galleon bound for Acapulco of its cargo of gold, silver, emeralds, and pearls. The *Golden Hind,* with at least a million dollars worth of loot in her hold, bobbed like a cork on the giant waves that rolled shoreward. Drake, who was at the top of Spain's list of most-wanted buccaneers, knew that all of the more heavily armed ships the Spaniards could muster would be watching and waiting for him to return to England by way of the Strait of Magellan. So he decided to sail north instead, hoping to find the mythical Northwest Passage which, he thought, would enable him to sail from the North Pacific across the top of the continent and out to the Atlantic Ocean. From there it would be a relatively easy trip home to England. But as he headed north he ran into mists, dense fog, strong winds, and rain. The sea broke on massive black rocks that loomed offshore. Navigation became extremely hazardous. Wisely, Drake changed his mind. He turned his ship about and headed south. He left the search for the Northwest Passage to others whose ships were laden with less precious cargo.

The *Golden Hind* dropped anchor in a well-hidden cove near Point Reyes in northern California. Like all wooden ships of that day, warped by tropical heat and pelted by raging seas, it needed repairs.

And Drake needed time to plan their homeward route. Fortunately, along with the treasure his ship carried were navigation charts used in piloting the Spanish galleons on their routes between Manila and San Blas or Acapulco on the Mexican coast. On July the twenty-third he set sail from his California hideout to cross the Pacific Ocean. The Spaniards were baffled. They had never dreamed that Drake would attempt such a dangerous voyage and escape the trap they had so carefully set.

Spain took little interest in the Pacific Northwest until her ambassador to the Russian court sent warnings of Russian plans to explore the North Pacific. Vitus Bering, a Dane in the service of Peter the Great, was ordered to sail into the seas off the coast of Asia. As a result of this expedition the Russians discovered Alaska. The sea-otter furs they found there stirred them to greater activity. The Spanish king, Carlos III, feared the Russian intruders would lay claim to lands that he felt were rightfully his. Urgent orders were sent to his viceroy in Mexico to dispatch ships to the North Pacific and to establish settlements along the coast.

In 1774 one of Spain's most experienced navigators, Juan Pérez, sailed from San Blas in the *Santiago* and headed north. He went as far as Alaska without landing along the way and then returned to San Blas with a good description of the coast, but with little else accomplished.

A year later two more Spanish ships, a frigate under command of Don Bruno Heceta and a smaller vessel under Juan Francisco de la Bodega y Quadra, left San Blas to explore the North Pacific. On this voyage Heceta went ashore near Point Grenville on the Washington coast to plant a cross and claim the land for King Carlos III. He came upon what seemed to him to be the mouth of a large river. However, his men, weakened by scurvy, were unable to launch a boat to investigate further, so Heceta sailed on and simply labeled the river Rio San Roque on his charts. This was the great river Yankee Captain Robert Gray was to discover years later and name after his ship, the *Columbia*. Quadra's expedition, which landed farther north, turned out to be an ill-fated one. A long boat from his ship took several crewmen to the beach at the mouth of the Hoh River to fill the ship's water casks. Indians ambushed them and massacred every man in the party. Quadra and the rest of his men escaped, however, and Quadra later became the Spanish governor of Nootka.

Captain James Cook, one of England's greatest navigators and geographers, sighted Yaquina Bay on the Oregon coast in the spring of 1778 and then proceeded north. His two ships, the *Resolution* and the *Discovery,* passed the mouth of the Columbia and the entrance to the Strait of Juan de Fuca. Both were hidden by drizzly rain and fog. Cook named the cape at the mouth of the strait Cape Flattery. His ships anchored in Friendly Cove, which he named Nootka Sound, for some time. Then Cook explored neighboring inlets and islands and made several landings to claim the region for King George III of England. While he searched for the Northwest Passage as Sir Francis Drake and many other explorers had done before him, the sailors on his ships bartered nails, buttons, and bits of metals with the Indians in exchange for sea-otter pelts. After he had explored the vicinity of Nootka Sound, Captain Cook ordered his ships north to the Aleutian island chain. In this northern region the short arctic summer was almost over. Cold weather forced him to turn south toward the Sandwich Islands (today's Hawaiian Islands) where the climate was more pleasant. During their stay in the Sandwich Islands a misunderstanding arose between Captain Cook and the natives. The great explorer was killed. His ships sailed on without him to Macao, the Portuguese colony on the coast of China. In these Oriental ports the sailors discovered the high value merchants had come to place on sea-otter pelts. The few they had obtained by bartering with the Indians on Nootka Sound brought fabulous prices. When they brought this information back to London with them, English merchants immediately outfitted vessels, put them under the command of traders, and sent them on the way to the Pacific Northwest to obtain a share of the fur trade.

A ship flying the flag of the new American republic, a flag not previously seen in the North Pacific, came out of the fog off Tillamook Bay one August day in 1788. The ship was the *Lady Washington* owned by Boston merchants and under the command of a young Yankee sea captain, Robert Gray. It sailed north along the coast to Nootka Sound, there to await the *Columbia,* a larger ship commanded by John Kendrick who headed the trading expedition. To the surprise of Captain Gray, Friendly Cove, an arm of Nootka Sound, was filled with ships belonging to English traders who were busy bartering with the Indians. After the *Columbia* reached the rendezvous two Spanish naval vessels arrived. Aboard was Don Estevan José Martinez, sent to Nootka at the request of the Spanish viceroy of Mexico. He had been ordered to establish a colony to thwart any attempts the Russians might make to claim the territory.

History-making events occurred during that winter of 1778-1779 on Nootka Sound. While he remained on friendly terms with the Americans, Martinez confiscated the property and some of the ships of the English on the claim that trading was being done in an area in which Spain had the exclusive right to the privilege. The ships, their officers, and crews were sent to the Spanish base at San Blas. Upon their arrival at San Blas, however, they were released on orders from the viceroy who knew what dangerous international implications Martinez's action had. In fact, when word of the incidents at Nootka reached London it brought England and Spain dangerously close to war. Fortunately, as tempers cooled, the controversy was settled by the agreement known as the Nootka Sound Convention of 1790, in which Spain agreed to make a settlement for the property seized and conceded the right of other nations to trade in the Pacific Northwest and to make settlements wherever she had not already done so.

Gray exchanged vessels with Kendrick in the spring of 1789. He loaded the *Columbia* with furs and sailed for China. Sale of the furs to Chinese merchants paid for a cargo of tea which Gray took to Boston. On arrival in Boston harbor Captain Gray received a "hero's welcome." The *Columbia,* with stars and stripes at her masthead, was the first American ship to circle the globe.

Captain Gray was sent on a second voyage to the Pacific Northwest in the *Columbia* in 1791. It was on this expedition that he sailed his ship into the mouth of the great river he named the Columbia. When Gray met Captain George Vancouver, an English sea captain on a mission to the Pacific Northwest, he mentioned his discovery of the river. As England's representative Vancouver was to carry out the terms of the Nootka Sound Convention through conferences with Quadra, the Spanish governor of Nootka. Despite lengthy discussions, however, Quadra and Vancouver could not come to agreement on some of the details of the settlement of the Nootka controversy. These were left for decisions by English and Spanish diplomats meeting in 1793 in Madrid. Meantime, Vancouver did spend much of his time searching for the nonexistent Northwest Passage and trying to determine whether the Strait of Juan de Fuca was the entrance to this long-sought waterway. He leisurely explored Puget Sound, the Strait of Georgia, and the coastal waters as far north as southeastern Alaska, which was occupied by the Russians.

During the same years that Captain Vancouver was probing into the inlets and bays of Puget Sound other brave men were experiencing severe hardships and exposing themselves to great danger in their attempts to reach the Pacific by an overland route from the interior of the continent. Some were searching for a river that would carry them

Captain Robert Gray discovering the Columbia River, a painting by Fred S. Cozgens

down the valleys of the western side of the mountain ranges to the coves and inlets the Spaniards and English had reached by way of the sea. One of these land explorers, Alexander Mackenzie, was in the service of the North West Company's post at Fort Chipewyan in the Athabaska region east of the Rockies. He had long dreamed of finding a way leading westward across the mountains to the sea. After desperate struggles with streams raging between high-walled canyons, difficult cliffside portages, and problems arising from travel through the territory of hostile Indians, he journeyed from the Fraser River to the Bella Coola in British Columbia and on to coastal inlets. On July 22, 1793, Mackenzie and his companions saw the open sea.

President Thomas Jefferson did much to get American explorers, traders, and others into the virtually unknown country west of the Mississippi River. To bolster American claims to the region, exploration, surveys and, eventually, settlements had to be made. Through Jefferson's efforts Congress appropriated funds to send an expedition to gather information and make contacts with Indian tribes which could prove valuable to American traders. Captain Meriwether Lewis and

Lieutenant William Clark were selected by President Jefferson to lead the expedition. They set out in May 1804, and both men kept detailed journals of the entire trip. With barge and canoes they started up the Missouri River. For much of the time some of the men walked along the bank of the stream making notes about the vegetation and terrain and hunting for game. By October the expedition reached the villages of the Mandan Indians in what is now North Dakota. Here they built a fort out of logs cut from cottonwood trees and called it Fort Mandan. The entire expedition spent the winter here and kept very busy making clothing, canoes, and other equipment and gathering information for the rest of their journey.

During the spring of 1805, they planned the routes they would take. Charbonneau, a Frenchman living with the Indians, was secured as an interpreter. His wife, Sacajawea, accompanied him and served as guide and interpreter. She was a Shoshoni Indian who had been taken captive by a Blackfoot tribe and sold as a slave to the Indians of the village in which Charbonneau lived. On April 7, 1805, the six canoes carrying the members of the expedition and supplies moved out onto the river.

The expedition would have to win the friendship of the Shoshoni Indians and would need their help in finding a way across the Rocky Mountains. Sacajawea, whose brother was a Shoshoni chief, was relied upon to win the help of this tribe. The expedition traveled through the Lemhi Pass and on to the edge of the Bitterroot Range. Their gateway through the Bitterroots to the west was by way of the Lolo Pass.

Many hardships and difficult situations faced Lewis and Clark along their route. Their journals tell of the frightened buffalo bull that charged into their camp one night in Montana. They were forced to live on dried salmon and roots, foods which the plateau Indians relished. And sometimes when they were famished and no other food was available they even had to eat dogs. They eventually reached the Pacific where they built Fort Clatsop near the mouth of the Columbia River and in what is now Oregon they settled down for the winter.

Fort Clatsop has been reconstructed and it is one of Oregon State's most interesting parks. The palisade, the living quarters for officers and men, and those for Charbonneau, Sacajawea, and their young son who was born after the expedition left Fort Mandan, have been furnished with rustic chairs, tables, and bunks which duplicate the original furniture made by the men at the time the fort was built. From the flagstaff flies a copy of the stars and stripes of that period. A trail shaded by trees leads to the canoe landing on a slough hidden by a dense growth of cattails. A dugout made exactly as the canoe makers of the expedition would have made it rests on the riverbank.

The return trip of the Lewis and Clark expedition during the summer of 1806 varied little from the route that was taken on the way west. At the Mandan villages several of the most important chiefs joined the group as Lewis had promised to take them to Washington to visit President Jefferson.

The Lewis and Clark expedition was of immense value to the United States. It proved that the Pacific could be reached by an overland route across the Rockies which many had thought was an impassable mountain barrier. Although explorers and trappers had been familiar with the land as far as the juncture of the Missouri and Yellowstone rivers, important discoveries were made beyond that point in regions where white men had never been. When the expedition arrived in St. Louis late in September 1806, the whole population of this frontier town turned out to greet them.

By 1806 American ships had won the major share of the trade with the Indians living near the coast in the Pacific Northwest. Only a relatively few English sea traders had come into the area. In that same year more than a hundred trappers left St. Louis to travel overland into the Rocky Mountains and the regions beyond them. In 1803, the United States had purchased the Louisiana Territory from France. This consisted of the land extending from the Gulf of Mexico to Canada and from the Mississippi River to the Rocky Mountains. The race between the English and the Americans for the furs and the control of the Pacific Northwest was under way.

The two large fur-trading companies, the Hudson's Bay and the North West Company, with posts in the prairies and the central lakes region of the continent, lost no time in sending their traders and trappers into the Pacific Northwest. The Hudson's Bay Company, the older of the two, was English. Its headquarters were in London. The original title of this company in the charter granted by King Charles II of England in 1670 was "Governor and Company of Adventurers of England trading into Hudson's Bay." The North West Company, formed in the winter of 1783–1784, was primarily a Canadian company with its headquarters in Montreal. Many of the men who had worked for years for the Hudson's Bay Company joined the North West Company, particularly those men who were more interested in exploring and surveying unknown country than in developing trade with the Indians.

One of these men to leave the Hudson's Bay Company was David

Sketch of Fort George, Oregon

Thompson, who entered the service of the North West Company in 1797. In his service with Hudson's Bay, Thompson had found that his love of exploring was frowned upon and that he had no opportunity to pursue his interest in geography. Over the years with the North West Company, however, he was able to cross the Rockies several times, establishing trading posts and mapping the country through which he traveled. The accomplishment of which he was most proud was his survey of the Columbia River from its source to its mouth.

Simon Fraser, another North Wester, was also set on crossing the Rockies and traveling down the Columbia. He followed Mackenzie's route to the point where the Nechako River joins the Fraser, establishing trading posts as he went. One of the posts, which he named Fort George, was built at the juncture of the Nechako and what he thought was the Columbia. On May 28, 1805, his expedition started out in four canoes down the river which bears his name today. The canoes were badly damaged in raging rapids and were thrown from whirlpools up against canyon walls. In the most dangerous places portages had to be made; the men moved along steep canyon walls by clinging to ladders made of poles, a device used by the Indians. After many days of tortuous travel Fraser and his men neared the river's mouth, about where the city of New Westminster is today. Hostile Indians prevented them from going farther. Much to Fraser's disappointment, observations he made checked in no way with the description of the lower reaches of the Columbia that Gray had discovered. He had, in fact, journeyed down the Fraser rather than the Columbia.

A shrewd New York merchant, John Jacob Astor, had for several years purchased furs from the North West Company in Montreal and sold them at a considerable profit to customers in Europe. The demand for beaver pelts had become greater than that for sea-otter furs, so Astor decided to extend the operations of his American Fur Company to the Pacific Northwest. He took into his association some of the men who had had long experience with the North West Company and formed the Pacific Fur Company. In 1810, Astor sent two expeditions to the mouth of the Columbia, one by land and the other by sea. The group that sailed aboard the *Tonquin* under the command of Captain Jonathan Thorn reached its destination first, in 1811. This unfortunate expedition was to meet with disaster. Shortly after landing some of the crew and part of the supplies, the *Tonquin*'s captain sailed away on a trading expedition. The ship was lost at sea and the men he left on land were massacred by the Indians. Shortly thereafter a second ship was dispatched from New York and it arrived safely with more men and supplies. The land expedition crossed the continent, following the trail of Lewis and Clark. They did not arrive until February 1812, because of the difficulties encountered on their trip. Astor's fort and settlement became known as Astoria.

Astor's dream of a trading empire on the Pacific was doomed to failure. With the outbreak of the War of 1812 between the United States and England the partners in his venture sold Astoria in 1813 to the North West Company. A British warship stood off Astoria ready to take possession of the fort and the surrounding country. The peace treaty signed at the end of the war, however, required that all property and territory which had been seized must be returned to its owner. Thus the land on which Astoria was built became American territory again. By this time, Astor had understandably lost his enthusiasm for a trading empire in the Pacific Northwest and was content to restrict his activities to his trade in furs in regions east of the Rockies.

The quest for furs now became a war between the two great companies, Hudson's Bay and the North West Company. So bitter did the rivalry become that the British government insisted the two companies merge. This was done in 1821 and the name Hudson's Bay Company was retained.

The new company sent George Simpson to the Pacific Northwest to bring about changes it felt would improve trade in the region and to establish rules to make the work done at each post more effective. He ordered that Fort George at Astoria be abandoned and that a new post, Fort Vancouver, be built about one hundred miles up the Columbia River. He appointed Dr. John McLoughlin to be chief factor of the new post with orders to prevent the advance of American trappers into the region. Posts were also built at Fort Langley on the Fraser River in British Columbia and Fort Nisqually on an inlet in the southern part of Puget Sound. Later other forts were established in the Columbia Basin and Idaho.

For a couple of decades there were rich harvests of beaver pelts and then the fur supply dwindled rapidly. Sea otters, ruthlessly slaughtered as sea traders combed coastal Indian villages bartering for their silky pelts, were so scarce by 1828 that the search came slowly to a halt. Late in the 1840s beavers began to disappear. Intensive trading and trapping left empty beaver homes of sticks and mud in marshes and creeks that once had swarmed with these animals. Eventually the forts which had been built to serve as headquarters for the fur trade were either abandoned or became stations where emigrants to the area could purchase provisions and equipment.

As this period of adventurous fur trading drew to a close one of the most colorful figures in the early history of the northwest disappeared from the scene. The French-Canadian voyageurs no longer paddled their big canoes along the region's lakes and streams. Their lusty shouts and singing ceased to echo through the valleys. Their arrival at the trading posts to which they brought supplies or cargoes of pelts had always been a gala event.

In the thirties of the same century missionaries came to the region. Some came west with bands of trappers from St. Louis. In 1832 a delegation of Indians traveled to St. Louis to ask that missionaries be sent to their people to teach them about the white man's God and the Bible. Jason Lee, a young Methodist minister, and his nephew, David Lee, were the first to respond. Lee built the mission in the forest of the Willamette valley in 1834. It proved to be of greater service to the settlers who came to the valley than to the Indians. Jason Lee felt that these people needed help in easing their hardships and loneliness. He appealed to Congress to give them the benefit of American laws and government, and helped them to till the soil and grow crops. The makeshift agreement which resulted from the War of 1812, and provided for joint occupancy of the Oregon Country by both American citizens and British subjects, had proved far from satisfactory. The settlers wanted title to the land on which they built their homes and protection from lawless individuals who had come into the region. The British government gave the Hudson's Bay Company authority to handle these and other problems for British subjects. The United States government, however, left all problems to be solved by the settlers themselves.

In 1836, the American Board of Commissioners for Foreign Missions sent Dr. Marcus Whitman and Henry Spalding and their wives out west. There was no Oregon Trail at this early time, and so they followed the trails used by Indians and traders until they reached Fort Vancouver. There, Chief Factor John McLoughlin invited the women to remain as guests of the company until the missions were ready. Whitman established his mission among the Cayuse Indians at Waiilatpu, the "Place of the Rye Grass," near the present city of Walla Walla. It eventually grew to include an adobe house, a gristmill beside a pond, a blacksmith shop, and other buildings. An irrigation canal carried water from the millpond to fields where corn, grain, and vegetables were grown. Spalding built his mission among the Nez Percé Indians at Lapwai near the site of present-day Lewiston, Idaho. After 1842 emigrant wagon trains began to make the mission at Waiilatpu a stop on the way west. Weary travelers found the mission a welcome place to rest, to replenish supplies, and to make repairs before proceeding to the Willamette valley.

Whitman developed an alphabet for the Cayuse language, obtained a small printing press for the mission, and printed Cayuse translations of books. Most of the Cayuse Indians, however, showed little interest in the Bible or in accepting the help of Whitman and his wife in teaching them to read and grow their own food.

There were several reasons for a growing suspicion on the part of the Indians. The ever increasing influx of settlers into their lands worried them. Their camas prairies were being overrun by grazing cattle. Animals upon which they depended for food were being trapped or hunted by the white man to such an extent they were becoming scarce. The buffalo herds they hunted on their expeditions to the Snake River plain or the plains of the upper Missouri valley were rapidly becoming smaller. Measles brought by emigrants in 1847, to which the Indians had little or no resistance, wiped out a large part of the Cayuse tribe.

Resentment and suspicion reached a peak in the autumn of 1847. A band of disgruntled Cayuse warriors attacked the Waiilatpu mission, killing Dr. Whitman, his wife, and several others. They took a large number of women and children captive. These prisoners were later released through the efforts of Peter Skene Ogden of the Hudson's Bay Company. The ruins of the building foundations and the millpond are all that remain of the mission at Waiilatpu today. A memorial shaft has been erected on the site. The Whitman Mission National Historic Site is maintained by the National Park Service.

The massacre brought an end to the missionary work sponsored by the American Board in the Oregon Country. It shocked Congress into action. In 1848 laws and government were created for the territory. On August 13, 1848, the bill creating the Territory of Oregon passed the Senate by a margin of a couple of votes. A few days later President James Polk appointed General Joseph Lane governor of the territory.

Oregon Territory included the present states of Oregon, Idaho, and Washington plus parts of Montana and Wyoming. Oregon City became the territorial capital. In 1851 the capital was transferred to Salem. Federal troops were sent to forts in the region immediately and Governor Lane started west to take up his new assignment.

It was not long before settlers living north of the Columbia began to find it inconvenient to have to travel all the way to Salem in order to reach the capital of the new territory. They held a convention at Monticello near the mouth of the Cowlitz River in 1852 and sent a memorial to Congress seeking a division of Oregon Territory. They recommended that a Territory of Columbia be created. The legislature in session in Salem did the same. In 1853 Congress passed a bill which granted the request but named the new territory Washington rather than Columbia. Isaac I. Stevens was appointed governor. Washington Territory included what is now Washington State plus the panhandle of Idaho and part of Montana. In 1859 Oregon as we know it today was granted statehood. And, in 1890, the state of Idaho was created and given the boundaries it now has. Washington became a state in 1889.

Settlement and Indian Wars

BEFORE the wagon trains began rolling westward from Independence, Missouri, less than two hundred people other than Indians lived in the Oregon Country. Most of these were Hudson's Bay Company employees, missionaries, and trappers. The first large contingent of prospective white settlers, about one thousand strong, came during the migration of 1843. They were young families from the east who, discouraged by the severe depression of 1837, decided to try life in the new land west of the Rockies. The number of wagon trains and emigrants heading westward increased enormously in the 1840s. It has been estimated that from 1840 to 1850 more than fifteen thousand emigrants went west by way of the Oregon Trail. Some went on to California after crossing the Rockies, while others settled in different parts of the Pacific Northwest. Nearly fourteen thousand decided to make their home in the Willamette valley in Oregon.

The Willamette valley became the most populous area of the entire region. It offered many advantages. The climate was mild, and the necessities of life were readily available. The western headquarters of the Hudson's Bay Company was at Fort Vancouver which was close by and, through the kindness of its chief factor, Dr. John McLoughlin, supplies and equipment were easily obtained. The early settlers were very fortunate that McLoughlin was in charge of the Vancouver post. Because of his help, their first year in the new land was far more pleasant than it would otherwise have been. Among the settlers in the valley there were French-Canadians who had left the Hudson's Bay Company

Settlers traveling westward in a covered wagon train in 1866

to build a home and turn to farming. There were a few prospectors and miners who chose to give up the hardships of moving from one gold strike to another for a more secure future in farming. When the prices offered for pelts had dropped and fur-bearing animals became less plentiful some trappers also chose the region for their home. Since most of these men were married to Indian women they were reasonably safe from attacks by neighboring tribes. And, on the whole, the Indians in the valley and its vicinity were friendly, unlike those tribes farther away from Fort Vancouver.

The life and home of the Willamette valley settler were simple. There were none of the comforts to which most of these newcomers had been accustomed. Before sawmills were built to meet the demands for lumber, homes were built of logs. Spaces between the logs were chinked with moss mixed with clay or mud. Moss was plentiful in the moist climate of the Oregon Country. Some of the logs were split to form planks like those used by coastal Indians in building their plank houses. Cedar, a relatively straight-grained wood, was easily split with simple tools. Most of the cabins had earthen floors and their roofs were made by spreading willow boughs and covering them with clay. Window glass was hard to obtain. Some settlers ordered it through Hudson's Bay from London and usually had to wait a year for it to arrive. Most of the cabins had windows covered with deerskin treated with oil or muslin coverings. These were translucent so that they admitted light and yet objects could not be seen through them. Doors were made of logs or poles and, when the materials became available, they consisted of two parts. The upper part could be opened while the lower part remained closed. There was a definite advantage to these "Dutch doors" as they are called. Indians were naturally curious about the way the white people lived and did not hesitate to walk into a settler's home to watch the womenfolk preparing a meal or spinning wool. When the top half of the door was open the Indians could observe the settlers without entering the house and disturbing them.

The settler's home had furniture made from logs and poles. The logs were hewn or split to the form that was needed. Beds were terribly uncomfortable. The bedstead, built of logs, had a thick layer of straw or corn husks for a mattress and this was covered with blankets or buffalo robes. Most of the treasured furniture and luxuries that had

A typical pioneer cabin. This one has been reconstructed in Julia Davis Park, Boise, Idaho.

been packed in the wagons for the trip west were discarded along the trail as travel became more difficult. Loads had to be lightened as wagons broke down and oxen became footsore and weak. Feather beds and spinning wheels were the most valued possessions and the last articles to be left behind.

Clothing that had been brought west soon became worn and had to be replaced. Clothes were made of buckskin and homespun wool and the womenfolk, skilled in their use of knitting needles, used every spare moment to knit socks and scarves. Few of the settlers had stoves. Cooking was done in kettles over open fires in fireplaces built of stone. Water was filtered through wood ashes and the resulting alkaline solution was boiled with waste fats to obtain a soft soap used in washing work clothing. At night the firelight from the fireplace, flickering and dim, helped to light the cabin. For lamps the settlers used wicks set in pots of fish or whale oil. There were few books to be had but almost every home had a Bible.

More and more settlers continued to head west until, in the late 1850s, there were about thirty thousand of them in the Oregon Country. This was roughly five thousand more than the number of Indians. At this point, the government decided the Indians should live on reservations. It is not surprising that conflicts arose between the white man and the Indian. The Indian's use of vast areas merely for hunting was a waste of land needed for farms for the settlers, as far as the government was concerned. The Indians became furious when they were told they had to live on reservations. Governor Stevens, shortly after his arrival in Olympia, began making treaties with coast tribes in an attempt to convince them to abide with the government's policy. He also invited Joel Palmer, superintendent of Indian Affairs in Oregon, to join him in a council meeting at Walla Walla in May 1855, with tribes living east of the Cascades. About five thousand warriors with their squaws and children arrived arrayed in colorful finery. After two weeks of talking tribal chiefs signed treaties accepting the transfer to reservations, some reluctantly, and others with no intention of abiding by treaty terms. Additional council meetings were held at other sites. The Nez Percé were generally friendly and helpful. But on the whole, Indian resentment grew at the loss of much of their traditional hunting, digging, and fishing grounds. There was harassment of settlers and federal troops and an increase in the number of raids and massacres. There was even an attempted raid on Seattle. The serious Rogue River War broke out in southern Oregon in 1855, when certain tribes in southern Oregon and northern California refused to move to reservations. One of the Indian leaders was Chief John of the Shasta tribe. The war was marked by Indian raids on isolated white settlements, and by murders and attacks on stagecoaches and wagon trains. Troops were brought in to protect the settlers, prospectors, and travelers in the area. The war ended when Chief John lost the support of most of his tribesmen and surrendered.

Sporadic trouble with tribes in different parts of the northwest continued for twenty years or more. Young Joseph, chief of a Nez Percé band which had been given a reservation in the Wallowa Mountains by a treaty signed in 1855, found his people involved in trouble in 1876 due to arguments over the ownership of some cattle which culminated in the killing of an Indian by a settler. His band was ordered to vacate the Wallowa Mountain area and to go to the Clearwater reservation. Joseph convinced his people they should comply. But more trouble came when some of his young Nez Percé warriors killed a number of white settlers. This led to the battle in the canyon of the Salmon River near White Bird Canyon in which the Indians won a decisive victory over four hundred soldiers under General Oliver Otis Howard's command. Chief Joseph then moved his people over the Lolo Pass. His brilliant strategy won the admiration of the military men who eventually were successful in capturing him before he reached the Canadian border. He and his people, despite promises, were sent to a reservation in the midwest; and later, after several years, to the Colville Reservation in northern Washington.

Finally, after many years of resistance, the Indians realized further war against the white invaders of their lands was futile. With their hunting grounds overrun by settlers, their camas prairies converted to pastures or farmland, and their fishing rights restricted despite court battles to force adherence to treaty promises, they were gradually forced to adopt the white man's ways. Many today live on reservations. Many others live on farms and use farming methods learned from their white neighbors. In eastern Oregon and Washington some of the cattlemen owning or operating large ranches are Indians. In both Washington and British Columbia many have become commercial fishermen owning their own boats and equipment.

There has been a great desire among the more than thirty-four thousand Indians in the states of the Pacific Northwest to obtain an education. Schools are provided on reservations where the distance to public schools is too great and those Indians who do live in towns attend the public schools there. The number of Indians seeking an education has tripled since World War II.

Western Washington: Evergreen Country

WASHINGTON, the "Evergreen State," consists of two very contrasting parts. The Cascade Range runs from north to south to form a high mountain wall between them. To the west are forests of evergreen trees in a land with a climate so mild that snow rarely blankets its valleys and plains and grass remains green all through the winter. To the east of the range is a treeless plateau, green in summer, where irrigation canals supply water and pine forests cover the foothills and mountain ranges that form its rim. Where the irrigation canals do not reach and the pattern of farms fades away the land is splotched with a mosaic of the pastel colors of sagebrush, prickly-pear cactus, and tumbleweed. The eastern part of the state has much colder winters than the west with frequent snow and its summers are dry and very warm. The entire state covers 66,709 square miles—slightly less than Missouri and almost nine times the area of Massachusetts. Within its borders live three million people. Canada lies to the north, Idaho to the east, and Oregon to the south of the state. The western border of the state is the rugged coast lashed by breakers that roll in from the Pacific.

There are no large rivers in the western part of the state but there are many relatively short streams like the Cowlitz, Lewis, Skagit, Duwamish, and Green rivers. Indian place names not easy to pronounce like Humptulips, Puyallup, Skamokawa, and Skykomish are sprinkled generously over a map of the region.

Vancouver, across the Columbia from Portland, Oregon, is the oldest settlement in western Washington. It began in the 1820s as Fort

Vancouver, the western headquarters of the Hudson's Bay Company, and grew into a very large trading post. After the Oregon Country became American territory, Fort Vancouver, in 1848, became a United States Army post. The town of Vancouver, which grew around the site of Fort Vancouver, has become the largest town in southwest Washington. Its nearness to the city of Portland, reached by way of an interstate bridge which spans the Columbia, has hampered its growth. Too many people prefer to live in Oregon's big city, where there is no sales tax!

A rolling plain extends north from Vancouver to Olympia, capital of the state. It is patterned with farms and small towns many of which began as a cluster of buildings around the camp and cookhouse of some logging operation years ago. West toward the Pacific are the Willapa Hills, the Grays Harbor area, and the driftwood cluttered seashore that ends where North Light tops Cape Disappointment to mark the north bank of the mouth of the Columbia. Northward from Olympia are the inlets and islands of Puget Sound reaching to the picturesque San Juan archipelago. West of the sound lies the sparsely settled Olympic Peninsula. In the heart of this peninsula is the huge Olympic National Park, a practically untouched wilderness paradise that can be explored only on foot or by pack horse over a network of trails. Roads have been built only short distances into the park as far as Hurricane Ridge, Sol Duc Hot Springs, and Lake Crescent and along two rivers on the west. This is the land where big herds of Roosevelt elk graze and long strands of moss draped from the trees of its "rain forests" sway above the damp spongy forest floor carpeted with moss and ferns.

Farms, lumber mills, and fish boat moorings are characteristic of the southwest. Longview, between Vancouver and Olympia, is the state's first planned city. Its colonial-style buildings, quiet tree-shaded streets and small man-made lakes in the heart of its business district contrast sharply with its huge lumber mills humming with activity and its bustling harbor on the Columbia packed with log booms. Aberdeen and Hoquiam on Grays Harbor are busy lumber-mill towns. Cloudy weather and drizzly rain occur so frequently in this lumber-mill country that residents of other parts of the Evergreen State speak jokingly of the croaking frogs of its lowlands as "Aberdeen canaries." Shelton, located a short distance to the east on an inlet of Puget Sound, holds its annual Forest Festival in the late spring. The celebration features log-rolling contests and other activities associated with the life of the logger. Thousands of Christmas trees are grown on tree farms in the area and, when November rolls around, the harvest begins. The cut trees are loaded aboard freighters bound for Hawaii, Venezuela, and other distant markets.

The beaches of southwest Washington are an attraction for clam diggers when very low tides occur in June and for fishermen during most of the year. The town of Westport prospers when its harbor is crowded with pleasure craft and fish boats. The long, hard sand beaches of the area are the best for those seeking razor clams. During clamming season hundreds of cars from Tacoma and Seattle bring whole families armed with buckets and clam shovels to take part in the harvest. Other varieties of clams can be found, but the delicious, meaty razor clam is the kind most eagerly sought. Commercial oyster beds in this region have been yielding big crops for years. Unfortunately, the pulp and paper mills which have gone up in the area have proven harmful to the oyster industry. Studies are being made to find ways of reducing their adverse effects on the oyster beds.

Wild cranberries grow in the peat bogs of the lowlands around both Long Beach and Grays Harbor. The environment is ideal since the bogs are large and are covered with sphagnum moss. Late in the last century a large tract near Long Beach was planted with vines brought from the Cape Cod country on the Atlantic coast. Some years

Cranberries are harvested in the Long Beach area of the Washington coast by the "wet pick" method.

later cranberry bogs were developed at Grayland near the entrance to Grays Harbor. The Grayland bogs cover an area several miles long. Two common methods of harvesting are used. Wet picking is done in the Long Beach area by flooding and then "beating the bogs" with a water reel that operates somewhat like an egg beater. It churns the water to free the berries from the submerged vines. The great masses of red berries then floating on the surface are pushed to collecting points by water booms very much like the booms used to raft logs on rivers. The other method, dry harvesting with picking machines, is used in the Grayland bogs.

Puget Sound is the inland sea of Washington which is linked with the Pacific by the Strait of Juan de Fuca. Small picturesque villages, mill towns, and farms pattern many of its islands. Some of the islands are still covered with forests. Captain Vancouver was the first to carry out an extensive charting of this inland sea when he explored its bays and inlets as far south as the present site of Tacoma in May and June, 1792. He named the sound after Peter Puget, one of the men who accompanied him on the voyage. The names he gave to many of its islands and bays and neighboring landmarks are still on present-day maps.

The small towns of the Puget Sound country surrounding the large ports of Seattle and Tacoma are on the shores of picturesque inlets. One such town is Bremerton, the site of the big naval base with dry-docks large enough to accommodate the airplane carriers of the Pacific fleet. The town swarms with officers and sailors of the ships in port for a routine overhaul or repairs. Ferries shuttle back and forth from Bremerton to Seattle. A highway leading from Bremerton to Tacoma crosses the high span of the Narrows Bridge. This is the bridge that replaced the one which came to be known as "Galloping Gertie" and made the headlines when it fell into the sound in 1940 during a wind storm.

The state capital, Olympia, lies at the southern tip of the sound. It is dominated by the imposing white dome of the capitol building looming above the gardens, fountains, and office buildings of other state departments.

The first American settlers on Puget Sound came by canoe and by fur traders' trails to its southern tip in 1845. They founded the little town of Tumwater. November 1851, saw a group of twelve adults and twelve children from Portland arrive aboard the schooner *Exact* and settle on Elliott Bay. They named the settlement of log cabins they built "New York–Alki," later shortened to "Alki," which, in Indian

Aerial view of Tacoma, Washington, with Mount Rainier in the background. The channel in the middle foreground is the City Waterway, one of seven inlets into Tacoma's industrial area from Commencement Bay on Puget Sound.

jargon, means "by and by." At this time San Francisco, booming after the rush for gold in the Sierras, was badly in need of logs for lumber for more buildings and piling for additional docks. When a sailing ship loomed offshore on a voyage seeking timber for the California market the settlers at Alki cut trees on their claims to supply the cargo. However, shallow water off Alki Point made it difficult to load the ships. So the following year, in 1852, the Alki settlers moved to a new location on the north side of Elliott Bay where the water offshore reached to greater depths. They named their new settlement Seattle in honor of Chief Sealth of the neighboring Duwamish Indian tribe who had been helpful and friendly to them.

Sailing vessels came to Puget Sound for lumber in ever increasing numbers in the 1850s. New towns sprang up near stands of tall timber by the water. At the north end of long narrow Kitsap Peninsula, which extends almost the full length of the sound, Port Gamble became a major world lumber port. Today fishing boats and pleasure craft tie up in the harbor in front of Port Gamble's steep-roofed New England-type houses that once looked out upon four-masted schooners being docked.

In 1856 Port Gamble was the scene of an incident that brought fear to the settlers in the region. A band of Haida Indians from north of the Canadian border came into the sound in their swift war canoes. They swooped down into the southern part of the sound frightening settlers with their muskets as they went. They then camped near Port Gamble and arrogantly refused to leave. Ships with howitzers moved in and a battle ensued in which the Indians suffered a loss in lives as well as canoes. Finally, they surrendered. The Indians were taken north aboard one of the ships and set free in their own territory off the British Columbia mainland.

In 1961 the Hood's Canal Floating Bridge was opened to traffic. It spans the entrance to the eighty-mile-long inlet at its entrance just south of Port Gamble. Unlike other floating bridges in the state, it is designed so that it can adjust to changes in the water level which fluctuates with low and high tides.

The city of Everett, about twenty-five miles north of Seattle, with a population of around forty-five thousand, has experienced several periods of boom and depression since its founding in 1862. Its pulp and lumber mills and docks at which cargo is handled for ships from many parts of the world have kept it prosperous in recent times. The most recent reason for boom in Everett was the building of a huge Boeing plant there which is producing the giant 747 jetliners.

Milking time is the major routine chore on the checkerboard of farms that form the hinterland of Bellingham. This northernmost city of the Puget Sound region with its more than thirty-five thousand people is spread along the shores and low hills encircling Bellingham Bay. When Captain Vancouver discovered and named this arm of the sound a dense forest of firs extended from the water's edge to the mountains. Over the years logging has erased the forest and the logged-off stumplands have been converted to farmlands. Log booms await cutting into lumber at the mills and fish canneries pack the haul of the fleet that works in the fishing grounds in the Strait of Juan de Fuca and beyond.

The hurried pace of modern living has not reached the 172 islands of the San Juan archipelago. The three largest islands in the group, Orcas, San Juan, and Lopez, have several small towns each. Some of the other islands, however, have few farms and only cottages. And some of the islands are simply clusters of rocks and driftwood with perhaps a few trees, which have become convenient resting places for sea gulls. The San Juans are actually located above the entrance to Puget Sound; however, most Washingtonians think of them as included in the Puget Sound area. But technicalities matter little to the people who live on the San Juans. They are there to enjoy a quiet life on a small farm, in a beachside cottage, or in a small community with little more than one general store. State ferry boats, winding their way along narrow channels, serve the larger islands. Chartered seaplanes are also a means of transportation to the mainland. Orcas Island, with Moran State Park and Mount Constitution, is the largest of the group. Friday Harbor on San Juan Island is the largest town, although it has less than a thou-

The San Juan Islands, Washington

sand inhabitants, and the site of the University of Washington Oceanography Laboratory.

In the 1850s an incident on San Juan Island almost sparked a war between Britain and the United States. Since the only casualty was a pig, historians often refer to it as the Pig War. Confusion over which of two channels marked the border extending from the forty-ninth parallel around the tip of British Vancouver Island was the basis of the trouble. The crisis was brought on when a pig belonging to a British subject residing on San Juan Island was shot by an American resident because it rooted up his potato patch. Officials in Victoria threatened to arrest the American. British naval vessels appeared offshore. American ships landed soldiers. The British landed marines. Eventually joint occupancy of the island was agreed upon until the clause in the treaty regarding the location of the boundary could be clarified. Settlement was not made until more than a decade later. After each side presented its case, the decision was left to Emperor William I of Germany. He decided that San Juan Island should be American territory.

Point Roberts, projecting from the mainland north of the San Juans, is an example of the strange consequences that sometimes result when treaties are made. When the forty-ninth parallel became the boundary between the United States and Canada it was drawn to the center of the Strait of Georgia, cutting across the neck of Point Roberts. The land below the border became American territory. The area of Point Roberts is only ten square miles and its population about two hundred. Water surrounds the point on three sides; the only land connection is with Canada. It is necessary, when traveling by car or bus, to go through Canadian territory to reach this tiny bit of the United States. Thus, an American resident of Point Roberts on a shopping trip to Blaine, the first American town across the border, must check four times with customs officials before he arrives home.

Larger, busier islands lie to the south of the San Juan archipelago in Puget Sound. The nearest is Fidalgo Island. Anacortes is its largest town with plywood and wood-processing plants, fish canneries, and a huge refinery that uses crude oil from the Canadian and Californian fields. A bridge that spans wild rushing waters links Fidalgo with Whidbey, a thirty-mile-long island of small chicken ranches and dairy farms. Outside its one town, Coupeville, stands a log blockhouse built by settlers to protect themselves during Indian uprisings many decades ago. Today this is a reminder of the insecurity of living in the region in those early times.

The harbor of Port Townsend, at the entrance to Puget Sound, was once crowded with sailing ships from all parts of the world and canoes from neighboring Indian villages. After the discovery of gold in the sand bars of the Fraser River ships brought the precious metal to this port. The city of Port Townsend boomed and its citizens dreamed of it as the leading city of the Pacific Northwest. They based their hopes on a transcontinental railroad that would lead to its door. Imposing stone buildings were built along its main street and elegant mansions crowned the cliff above the harbor. Streetcars rumbled along tracks laid in wide streets in its business district. Port Townsend became a busy place, but the railroad never materialized. For years the city thrived as the headquarters of the customs district, the port of entry for Puget Sound. But when that was moved to Seattle the streets of Port Townsend became quiet and some of the Victorian-style buildings and homes were vacated. Fortunately, however, Port Townsend never became a ghost town because its people never lost faith in its future. A large paper and pulp mill now provides its largest payroll. Victorian mansions, waterfront streets with "shanghai tunnels" beneath them through which drugged sailors were rushed to ships short of crews, art displays, and a summer school of the arts have attracted visitors in recent years. In Port Townsend and in neighboring Sequim there are more sunny days per year than in any other part of western Washington.

A few small towns are strung along the north shore of the Olympic Peninsula between Port Townsend's neighbor, Port Angeles, and the Makah Indian Reservation on Cape Flattery. Port Angeles is a younger city than Port Townsend, although the spot which became the site of the city was named as early as the eighteenth century by Don Francisco Eliza, the Spanish explorer who called it Puerto de Nuestra Señora de Los Angeles which means Port of Our Lady of the Angels. Lumber and pulp mills helped Port Angeles grow to a population of more than fifteen thousand.

Cape Flattery pokes into the Pacific. In winter it bears the brunt of storms from the ocean which bring drenching rains and high winds. The Makah Indians, descendants of the tribes that hunted seals and whales far out at sea in long cedar dugouts, live in the village of Neah Bay on Cape Flattery. When the menfolk are not out on the strait fishing for halibut or salmon they are busy mending their nets and other gear in preparation for a fishing expedition. Tatoosh Island, pounded by waves and drenched by rain much of the year, can be seen from Neah Bay.

All towns along the north and west shores of the Olympic Penin-

Majestic Mount Rainier and Tipsoo Lake in Mount Rainier National Park, Washington

sula are small. The 888,000-acre Olympic National Park occupies much of the land. There are no railroads or ports. The Olympic Loop Highway is the only way to get around the peninsula. The west coast is constantly exposed to storms and fog. The relatively narrow strip of land outside park boundaries has but two major industries, lumbering and fishing, both carried on on a relatively small scale. Restrictions on logging operations within Olympic National Park have eliminated large sources of timber. There is some small-scale cutting of timber in certain parts of the park under strict controls.

Forests of fir, cedar, and hemlock blanket the western slopes of the Cascade Range from the Canadian border south to the Columbia River in Washington State. Most of it is included within the boundaries of national forests. The preservation of forests and regions of scenic beauty is designed to insure recreational areas for now and the future.

Snow-capped Mount Baker, with smaller, more picturesque Mount Shuksan nearby, is a favorite recreation spot for Americans and Canadians.

Mount Rainier National Park is another popular recreation area. The peak was named by Captain Vancouver for his friend, Admiral Peter Rainier. Twenty-five of its glaciers have been named. Emmons Glacier, the largest, is four miles wide.

Other high snow-crested peaks lie farther south in the Cascades in western Washington. Mount St. Helens is seen best across Spirit Lake; Mount Adams, directly east, is reached by trails through a wilderness area. Both peaks are in Gifford Pinchot National Forest.

The climate west of the Cascade crest in both Washington and Oregon is moist and mild. Excessive rainfall occurs only in certain areas along the coast, particularly from Grays Harbor to Cape Flattery. When storms brew, warm moist air moves inland from the Pacific. As it rises to flow over the crest of the Olympics and the Coast Range it expands and cools. As it does so much of its water vapor condenses and falls as rain on the western slopes of these mountains and in nearby valleys. When the air moves down the eastern slopes to flow into the Puget Sound-Willamette trough it contracts and warms. This converts the rain to a drizzle or eliminates it altogether. As the air rises again to hurdle the Cascades it cools and brings rain to the foothills and peaks. It flows as relatively dry air down the east slopes to the Columbia Basin or the central Oregon plateau and desert. These areas are said to be in the "rain shadow" of the Cascades. This is the basic pattern of climatic influences in the region. Other factors can alter it to create local variations.

Normally, the winters are wet and the summers dry west of the Cascade crest. An average summer will be sunny and dry for two or three months; however, there have been years when the dry summer has lasted through October. Such a summer occurred in 1929 before the Grand Coulee and Bonneville dams, sources of hydroelectric power, had been completed. The power output of the hydroelectric plants serving Seattle and Tacoma dropped, and the Navy's aircraft carrier, the *U.S.S. Lexington,* had to be brought in to generate power for the two cities during late autumn and into December.

The high moisture content of the air over this part of the Pacific Northwest gives the climate a most desirable characteristic. There are very few electrical storms. It is unusual to hear thunder or see lightning more than twice a year.

Washington is a corner state. The ocean lies to the west. A foreign country lies to the north. On the east and south it borders states with no great concentration of population. This has affected the industrial development of the state. Until increased population brings about a greater demand for a more diversified industry, the major industrial plants will continue to be those associated with regional products. Lumber, plywood, and paper and pulp mills have been built. The abundance of fish and fruit has brought large food processing plants to the region. Wheatlands have brought flour mills. Extensive hydro-electric power supplies the needs of industries that depend upon electrolytic processes like the extraction of aluminum from its ores.

Eastern Washington: The Inland Empire

FROM THE CREST of the Cascades to the Idaho border and from Canada south to Oregon lies a land as different from the evergreen country west of the mountains as night is from day. It includes the heart of the Columbia Basin. This is eastern Washington.

In both prehistoric and modern times great changes have come to the eastern part of Washington State. Thousands of years ago deep coulees were cut into its surface at the close of the glacial period. Grand Coulee and Moses Coulee are the largest of these. Seventy-five years ago herds of wild horses raced across the sagebrush on the hills and plains near Ephrata. After the dawn of the present century nearly three thousand of these horses were rounded up, corraled, and shipped to South Dakota's badlands because they were ruining valuable grazing land which was needed for cattle. There are still a few of these wild horses left today. They live in the Horse Heaven Hills west of Richland and the Columbia River. These hills are too parched for dry farming and too high to benefit from irrigation, just as most of this region was before man made it otherwise, with his concrete, steel, and engineering know-how. The Grand Coulee Dam he built has already converted more than one and a third million acres of sagebrush country into fields of wheat, sugar beets, potatoes, peas, and alfalfa.

The Columbia River, curving its way across eastern Washington and then along the southern border of the state, is a major physical and economic feature. About five hundred miles of the "great river of the West" flow north of the Canadian border. Canal Flats in British

Columbia, where streams formed by the meltwater from Rocky Mountain glaciers join to make a slowly flowing rivulet, is sometimes given as the source of the Columbia. Others give Columbia Lake as the birthplace of this great river. Where it crosses the border into Washington and joins the Pend Oreille River its turbulent nature is calmed. Here, a little north of the town of Kettle Falls, is the upper end of the 150-mile-long Roosevelt Lake which is formed by the Columbia's water as it backs up behind the Grand Coulee Dam. Where once there were rapids and waterfalls there is now the slowly moving water of a long narrow lake with six hundred and sixty miles of shoreline.

An idea once suggested by William Clapp of Ephrata and widely publicized by Rufus Woods, editor of a Wenatchee newspaper, started

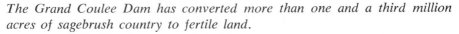

The Grand Coulee Dam has converted more than one and a third million acres of sagebrush country to fertile land.

engineers and economists thinking about the Grand Coulee Dam and the Columbia Basin project. Why not dam the river above the Grand Coulee where it turns north? Why not back up its waters for irrigation and, with electricity generated in the dam's powerhouses, pump water into a reservoir formed from its ancient ice age channel, the Grand Coulee? It would have to be a dam much larger than any man had made before. An intricate network of canals would carry water from the reservoir to a checkerboard of farms plotted in the heart of the Columbia Basin. New farms would be available for hundreds of people. By marketing the hydroelectric power much of the huge cost of the project would be defrayed over a period of years. Other ideas were offered. Verbal battles were frequent between proponents of each. Army engineers and Bureau of Reclamation experts made surveys, calculations, and lengthy reports. Then came the depression of the thirties. The federal government sought worthwhile projects to provide employment for a large work force. The Grand Coulee Dam proved to be a project which would fit perfectly into the Public Works Administration program. Preliminary work on the dam began in 1933 and contracts for the immense structure were signed in the summer of 1934.

The Grand Coulee Dam is huge, much larger than it appears to be in its vast setting of wide coulees and high canyon walls. It is 550 feet high and 4,173 feet wide. The base, built in the solid bedrock of the river channel, is a 500-foot-thick block of steel and concrete which tapers to a thickness of thirty feet at the top of the dam. Surplus electricity generated in the powerhouse at its base on the downstream side is used to pump water from Roosevelt Lake up two hundred and eighty feet to Banks Lake, a reservoir in the Grand Coulee. The reservoir was formed by blocking the Grand Coulee at both ends with earth-and-rock-fill dams. It is twenty-seven miles long. Water flows by gravity from the south end of Banks Lake into a network of canals and on to the farms in the Columbia Basin. There are more than two thousand miles of canals in the network. Water was let into these in 1952, to nourish the basin's six thousand square miles of farmlands. Rainfall provides the basin with from six to nine inches of water yearly, enough to quench the thirst of hardy sagebrush but only a fraction of the amount of water needed to grow the crops that are grown there today.

Although the Grand Coulee Dam was built primarily to supply water for the irrigation of new farms, the hydroelectric power it produces brought other changes to eastern Washington. It made possible the production of nuclear fuels for nuclear weapons. In 1943 a 640-square-mile tract of sagebrush, sand, and dry grass, green only where

Much larger than it appears in its vast setting of coulees and canyons, the Grand Coulee Dam is 550 feet high and 4,173 feet wide.

early irrigation projects had given rise to farm plots on the drab landscape, was taken over by the United States government. Residents of the sparsely populated area were moved out. On this big reservation the Hanford Engineer Works was built. Few knew its purpose. Those who did kept it a secret until its revelation would in no way impair the war effort or endanger security. When the story could be told it became known that the big reactors built at Hanford were bringing about the transmutation of uranium to polonium. This man-made element is a nuclear fuel for the atom bomb.

Richland, a small town on the Columbia near Kennewick and Pasco, became the administrative center of the Hanford Engineer Works, later called the Hanford Atomic Works. It was a trading center in a farming area that had profited from an early irrigation project which had brought water to the thirsty soil. Eventually a new Richland with wide streets, handsome office buildings, residences, and parks, replaced the original town. In recent years activity at Hanford Atomic Works has been curtailed somewhat. The end of World War II led to a decrease in polonium production but some reactors continue to produce that element for other purposes such as research in radio-biology, generating steam for the production of electricity, and the production of certain materials for peaceful uses.

The Columbia River, so completely harnessed by dams for irrigation, hydroelectric power, and flood control, has been almost entirely converted to a chain of long narrow lakes. No voyageur of fur-trading days would recognize the "great river of the west" today. Many of the sites of forts built in that era are now under water. The hordes of salmon so vital to the economy of the Nez Percé, the Spokanes, and other Indian peoples, can no longer migrate to the upper stretches of the river to spawn. The high man-made barriers have proven insurmountable to them. Fishways are a help to migrating fish only at low dams downstream. Towns have been inundated by water backing up and have either been moved to higher ground or been erased from the maps of the region. Kettle Falls, a few miles south of the Canadian border, replaces the Kettle Falls of pre-Grand Coulee Dam days, which is now under the waters of Roosevelt Lake. During the fur-trading era the Pacific Fur Company's Fort Okanogan was built near the mouth of the Okanogan River. Today its site is under the water backed up behind Chief Joseph Dam.

The people of the Pacific Northwest and experts at the Washington State Water Research Center generally oppose the proposal to divert Columbia River water to arid southwestern states such as Arizona. Proponents point to the 170 million acre-feet of the river's water which, they feel, is wasted as it flows into the Pacific annually. Those who object claim an aqueduct taking water from a point above the dams of the lower Columbia would endanger the flow required to produce hydroelectric power in a period of severe drought in the northwest. They do not wish to take this risk to satisfy Arizona's needs since a large part of her irrigation water is used to grow cotton, which requires an extensive amount of low-cost water. Other ideas have been offered to rule out this objection. One is to build a huge plastic pipeline to carry the water offshore undersea from some point between Bonneville Dam and the mouth of the river. Whether it is feasible to divert the Columbia's water southwestward, only the experts can decide. The problem is one which still requires extensive study and research before a solution can be found or a decision made.

Since the completion of the Grand Coulee several dams have been built on the Columbia between Sanpoil Bay and the bridge of one of the northwest's major highways which spans the Columbia at Vantage. Among these is Chief Joseph Dam, built primarily to generate electricity but which also plays a part in irrigation. As the Columbia now travels more leisurely along its way, the Nespelem, Okanogan, Methow, Twisp, Chelan, and Entiat rivers, all flowing between forested mountain ridges of the upper Cascades and the Okanogan Highlands, add their waters to the stream. The man-made lake behind Chief Joseph Dam reaches almost to Grand Coulee. It has been named Rufus Woods Lake to honor the Wenatchee editor who did so much to obtain approval of a high dam at the Grand Coulee. The Chelan River, shortest of the Columbia's tributaries in this part of eastern Washington, is the outlet for beautiful Lake Chelan. This lake lies in a deep trough gouged out of the eastern slope of the Cascades by a huge glacier. The town of Chelan is located at the southern end of the lake.

Wenatchee, a city of over seventeen thousand people, lies in a valley at the juncture of a river of the same name and the Columbia. When the thousands of apple trees in the orchards surrounding the town are in blossom, the city is host to hundreds of visitors who flock to join in its big annual celebration, the Washington State Apple Blossom Festival. Since the beginning of the century Wenatchee has been shipping apples to all parts of the world. At that time one boxcar of apples was shipped. In recent years the yearly average has been eighteen to twenty thousand carloads. In addition many carloads of fruits such as pears, peaches, and apricots are shipped out of Wenatchee each year.

The apple industry is based upon a thorough scientific study of what varieties should be grown, the best methods of protecting them from insect pests, and the most effective ways to harvest and store the crop. After the apples have been picked and washed part of the crop is stored in warehouses for shipment later in the year. The warehouse atmosphere is carefully controlled by decreasing the amount of oxygen, increasing the carbon dioxide content, and increasing the humidity so that the stored apples will keep their flavor and the skin will not shrivel. A temperature of thirty degrees Fahrenheit is maintained. The most popular varieties of apples in the Wenatchee valley are the Delicious and the Winesap, and the town's citizens are proud to have their city known as the "Apple Capital of the World."

Between Chelan and Vantage the Rocky Reach and Rock Island dams shackle the Columbia. Vantage is little more than a wide spot in the road, but near it is one of Washington's most interesting state parks, the Gingko Petrified Forest. The park covers sagebrush covered slopes and its museum overlooks the Columbia. Logs from trees that fell into water with a high content of dissolved minerals millions of years ago were buried and preserved under layers of lava. In the process of becoming petrified the minerals in solution in the water crystallized as insoluble solids as the wood decomposed. By this slow process a log of wood eventually became a log of stone with the pattern of rings found in the original faithfully reproduced. Although petrified wood originating from many different kinds of trees has been identified, that of the prehistoric Gingko tree predominates. Gingko trees do not grow in Washington today, but there is a modern variety found in the Orient.

Just above the bend of the Columbia in southeastern Washington the river receives the waters of the Yakima and Snake rivers. This is near the tri-city area which includes Richland, Kennewick, and Pasco. Richland is the "Atomic City"; Kennewick, the trading center in a region of large vineyards of Concord grapes and of cherry orchards; Pasco, a city with railroad repair shops surrounded by farms which grow wheat as the major crop. A familiar sight in these and most of the towns in this part of Washington are big grain elevators located beside railroad sidings. Beyond Pasco the Columbia turns sharply to the west to flow into man-made Lake Wallula formed by the river's waters backing up behind McNary Dam farther downstream. In the remaining two hundred and seventy-five miles of its course to the sea the Columbia is the Oregon-Washington state line.

The North Cascades of eastern Washington is an unspoiled wilderness. In the heart of it lies the Glacier Peak Wilderness Area, a wonderland of glaciers, alpine meadows carpeted with wild flowers in summer, and a system of trails along many of its mountain ridges which offers the hiker magnificent views across the Cascade Range. Glacier Peak, its summit at 10,528 feet, is almost as high as the more easily accessible Mount Baker to the northwest. There are countless peaks with patches of snow during summer in the North Cascade area. Trails wind between clumps of wind-twisted alpine trees and slopes matted with heather, but no roads penetrate this wilderness. This is one of the areas which conservationists have battled to save from those who would open it for mining and unrestricted timber operations.

Many of the towns in the north Cascades originated as coal mining or lumber mill settlements. Cle Elum and Roslyn began in this way. Orchards of apple and apricot trees in the valleys and on the foothills around Leavenworth, Cashmere, Omak, and Okanogan make a big contribution to the fruit crop of eastern Washington. Cashmere is the home of delicious fruit confections known as aplets and cotlets. Near the town is the Carey Historical Museum with its pioneer village for which buildings have been brought from many parts of the state. One of the buildings to be reconstructed is the old Cashmere mission built late in the last century by Catholic priests.

Ellensburg and Yakima are typical western towns on the edge of the Cascades. Ellensburg has a population of about nine thousand; Yakima, about forty-five thousand. Beef cattle are raised on the grazing land in the vicinity. Farmers of the outlying wheatlands make Ellensburg their trading center. Late each summer the Ellensburg rodeo brings cowboys, Indians, and whiskered prospectors to the town to take part in a revival of the days of the Old West. At harvest time Yakima is crowded with itinerant fruit pickers and harvest hands who come to work in the pear, peach, and apricot orchards and in the hopyards. In the hills west of Yakima is the Goat Rocks Wild Area; to the south, the big Yakima Indian reservation. With the great increase in land made productive through irrigation a large acreage is devoted to the growing of sugar beets. A sugar refinery is operating in Toppenish, south of Yakima, and another at Moses Lake in the heart of the Columbia Basin. The Gifford Pinchot National Forest, the Yakima Reservation, and some barren sagebrush and bunch-grass country fill most of the very sparsely settled triangular area between the Yakima River, the Columbia, and the crest of the Cascades.

The southeastern corner of Washington bounded by the Palouse and Snake rivers, the Idaho border, and the Oregon state line, is a country steeped in the history of the Old West. It is rich in tales of Indian raids, stagecoach holdups, and gun fights with desperadoes. Today it is a land where beef cattle graze and rolling hills are carpeted in late summer with fields of ripening grain. The Palouse Hills are blanketed with a patchwork of yellow, when wheat is ready to harvest. This part of eastern Washington has approximately fourteen inches of rainfall annually, enough to permit dry farming. The soil is cleared of sagebrush and bunch grass, tilled, and it still retains enough moisture to grow wheat. In regions where eight to twelve inches is the average annual rainfall, irrigation is required. Around the city of Walla Walla irrigation provides water for the thirsty soil and a large variety of crops are grown, including field peas and asparagus.

Walla Walla was the end of the trail for many emigrants who came in covered wagons. Its mild winters and frequent sunny days appealed to them. In the early 1870s, Dorsey S. Baker, a pioneer, built Washington's first railroad between Walla Walla and the Columbia River. It was made of fir timbers capped with iron strips and tied to the rail-

A combine harvests wheat in eastern Washington

road ties with rawhide. The story is told that in winter when the rawhide became wet and soft hungry wolves chewed it away. For several years the grain the railroad carried as freight made the venture highly profitable.

Today Walla Walla is a city of some 25,000 people. Its streets are shaded by elm, locust, and sycamore trees. Its name prompted Al Jolson to remark that it was a city its people liked so well they named it twice. Many Walla Wallans work in canneries, food-processing and meat-packing plants, and the chemical manufacturing industry. Ritzville, Dayton, Pomeroy, Colfax, and Pullman are smaller towns in the wheat-growing country between Walla Walla and Spokane.

Spokane, largest city of eastern Washington and second largest in the entire state, began as a settlement at the falls of the Spokane River in 1871. Today it has two hundred thousand people and the falls lie in the heart of the business district. Indians once flocked to this spot during salmon migrations to fish, talk, and trade. The name "Spokane" is an Indian word which means "children of the sun." The tables and outdoor fireplaces among the shade trees of Riverside Park provide pleasant picnicking sites. Lilacs are grown throughout the city and at the peak of their blossoming time the annual Lilac Festival is held. So much of the wealth in silver, gold, lead, zinc, and other metals mined in the mountains of the Idaho panhandle flows through Spokane that it is generally recognized as the mining center of the Pacific Northwest. Its flour and lumber mills and the agricultural productivity of the Okanogan valley make Spokane the "Capital of the Inland Empire."

Aerial view of Spokane Washington, the "Capital of the Inland Empire"

Western Oregon: The Promised Land

IN THE 1840s two settlers dreamed of building a big city in western Oregon's Willamette valley. They acquired a large tract of land near the juncture of the Willamette River and the Columbia. Francis Pettygrove, originally from Portland, Maine, and Asa Lovejoy who hailed from Boston spent less than one hundred dollars for it. A city was platted. It was hoped that some day it would extend far beyond both banks of the Willamette. Several streets were laid out between the river and the hill known now as Council Crest. A few houses, a couple of churches, and a school were built. Both men wished to name the city after his hometown. A flip of a coin broke the deadlock. Pettygrove won. In 1851, with approximately one thousand inhabitants, Portland became an incorporated town. When a steam mill was built some streets became skidroads down which oxen dragged logs to be cut into lumber. Farsighted businessmen had the Willamette dredged where it joined the Columbia so that ocean-going vessels could anchor there to load lumber, fruit, and cured salmon. Portland continued to grow despite the rush to California when gold discoveries were made. In fact, the gold rush eventually proved to be a boon to Portlanders. Californians needed the wheat and lumber which Portland could provide.

Oregon City, provisional capital of Oregon until 1852, is built on two levels. A free municipal elevator lifts pedestrians from the lower business district on the east side of the river to the cliff top ninety feet above overlooking the falls. Less than ten thousand people live in this

The Oregon state capitol in Salem

historic town today. Dr. John McLoughlin built a home here to which he retired in 1845 when he left the employ of the Hudson's Bay Company. Today, moved from its original location to McLoughlin Park, his home has been furnished as it was in the days when the kindly Hudson's Bay chief factor lived in it and has been made a national historic site.

Salem, the present capital, is fifty miles south of Portland on the Willamette. The huge statue of the pioneer, gleaming with the gold leaf which coats its surface, stands atop the fluted cylinder of white marble that is the heart of the capital. It can be seen at a distance of several miles from the city. Salem was built on the site of the Methodist mission which had been established there by Jason Lee.

The Willamette valley is the largest and richest in western Oregon. Its fields produce big crops of strawberries, raspberries, and loganberries. Pears, plums, and cherries ripen in its orchards. The dark Bing cherry, a favorite variety, was developed by an Oregon fruit grower. Among the farms spread across the valley floor are a few large towns, all of which have a lumber or plywood mill and most of which have food-processing plants for canning or freezing the local fruit and vegetable produce. Sheep and large herds of dairy cattle graze on the pasturelands. Oregon is one of the nation's major wool producers. Albany, farther up the valley, is a center for grass seed production and the extraction of oil from mint leaves by steam distillation. Eugene, the state's second largest city with a population of about fifty thousand, is the home of the University of Oregon. A rival college town about forty miles from Eugene is Corvallis, home of Oregon State University, in the heart of a dairy region. Just before the Thanksgiving and Christmas holidays McMinnville is one of the busiest towns in the valley. That is the season when truckload after truckload of turkeys from surrounding farms go to market. This town lies in the heart of a region with a large acreage devoted to growing walnut and filbert trees. Oregon's walnut crop is usually several thousand tons a year; the filbert crop, about twice as large as that.

Few parts of the world have a coastline as rugged and beautiful as the three hundred miles of Oregon that border the Pacific. The highway skirting the coast all the way from Astoria in northern Oregon to Brookings just north of the California state line commands magnificent views of the sea. There are miles of sandy beaches sprinkled with starfish and sand dollars and, along the northern beaches, an abundance of clams and crabs. Where sand has been washed away by the breakers the underlying gravel exposes moonstones, water agates, jasper, bits of wave-polished petrified wood, and Oregon jade. Dozens of capes are clothed with the green of Sitka spruce and cedar and a ground cover of colorful plants like salal, rhododendron, and azalea. Gleaming white lighthouses perched high on rocky headlands warn ships of the dangerous waters close to shore. Southward the coast becomes increasingly rugged with long lines of giant monoliths buffeting incoming waves. At some points strong winds have swept sand inland to encroach upon oceanside forests of gnarled and twisted trees, forming the Oregon dunes. The state of Oregon has preserved much of its beauty by creating a chain of parks along a good part of the three hundred mile coastline with picnic areas and trails leading to picturesque coves.

The animals of the seashore and coastal waters are on display in this beachcomber's paradise. The tide pools are the homes of countless varieties of mollusks, crabs, sea anemones, sea carrots, and jellyfish. Crabbing and clamming are rewarding activities in several bays along the coast. Crab rings, pots, rakes, and forks are used to catch of the fishing fleet return to their home ports in Tillamook, Newport, Reedsport, or Coos Bay loaded with cargoes of salmon, halibut, and the large crabs that migrate shoreward from deep water to feed. Boats sole. Seals and sea lions which migrate from California or Mexico northward as far as Alaska make offshore rocks their resting areas and can be watched from shore. Their barking can be heard for miles. Near Florence there is a large cave which is home to a herd of a couple of hundred sea lions that can easily be observed.

The gales that create the mountainous waves which lash the Oregon coast in winter usually originate far to the north in the Gulf of Alaska and strike as far south as Cape Blanco. Enormous waves thundering shoreward damage lighthouses during severe storms. These fierce gales once took a heavy toll of ships in the years before today's effective devices for detecting approaching storms were developed. Many tales have been told about shipwrecks, hidden treasure, and mutiny. Some years ago huge blocks of beeswax were discovered buried in the sand on Nehalem Beach. It is believed that in the sixteenth or seventeenth century a Spanish galleon was driven off course during a storm and wrecked. The beeswax, used in those days for making can-

Sheltered bathing beaches at Ecola State Park in Oregon

dles and wax images is all that remains today of the supplies the galleon was carrying to the missions in the domains of the king of Spain. Pieces of teakwood from Chinese junks have also been found on Oregon beaches indicating that at some remote time the Chinese might have reached the area even before European vessels came to the New World.

There are only a few well-protected harbors on the Pacific in this region. Tillamook, Reedsport, and Coos Bay are the largest of these. Fish canneries and lumber mills are located in each. One of the world's largest cheese factories is in Tillamook, and Coos Bay is Oregon's largest port for loading lumber.

Craftsmen in southern Oregon produce a great variety of beautiful articles, among them bowls, trays, and souvenirs carved from myrtle-wood. The tree from which this wood is obtained is found in a relatively small region along the coast and in the adjacent river valleys. Several groves have been set aside as state parks. The myrtlewood tree is also found in the Holy Land.

Some of the finest stands of Douglas fir and ponderosa pine in the northwest are found today in the forests of southern Oregon. Also, in the extreme southwest, there are groves of giant redwood trees. In May and June the area is particularly beautiful when rhododendrons, azaleas, and wild lilacs bloom. Where the Coast Range and the Siskiyou Mountains meet there is unspoiled country. By way of Hellgate Canyon the Rogue River cuts through the mountains to reach the Pacific at Gold Beach, a small town so named because of the gold nuggets found in the gravel at the river's mouth. A forest trail skirts the narrow stream through the more than a million acres of Siskiyou National Forest. There are no roads. The region is a paradise for sportsmen fishing for salmon and steelhead trout.

Fifty miles from Grants Pass, formerly a stagecoach stop in the Siskiyous, are the fantastic limestone formations of Oregon Caves National Monument. Stalactites and stalagmites form the glistening columns of the caverns in Mount Elijah. Crystals encrusting these limestone formations were formed over a long period of time by the precipitation of minerals dissolved in soil water which seeps through rock layers and drips to the cavern floor.

There are several large towns in southern Oregon west of the Cascades. Roseburg is in the sheep-raising region of the Umpqua valley. Medford, crowded with itinerant fruit pickers and cannery workers at harvest time, is in the heart of a land of pear orchards. Ashland, with its lithia springs and authentic Elizabethan theater where the plays of its summer Shakespeare Festival are presented, lies at the edge

The lower falls of Oregon's Multnomah Falls in the Columbia River gorge

of the Siskiyou Mountains. All are farm-marketing centers. A few miles west of Medford is sleepy Jacksonville, once a rip-roaring mining community when gold was to be found in the Siskiyous. Many of the buildings where bearded miners, gamblers, and sheriff's deputies made local history are still standing.

The western slope of the Cascade Range in Oregon is almost entirely within the boundaries of national forests where fir, spruce, and hemlock predominate. These forests are the home of mule deer, bear, and other wildlife. The Oregon Skyline Trail follows the crest of the Cascade Range to the California line. North of Crater Lake the snow-capped peaks of Mount Hood, Mount Jefferson, and the Three Sisters rise high above the sea of trees. Very few towns can be found in this area.

The Columbia River gorge is the gateway through the range. State parks along the Columbia protect the many waterfalls that tumble from cliffs to pools where ferns, salal, Oregon grape, and moss cover the forest floor. Multnomah Falls, 620 feet high, plunges from a cliff top in two leaps.

Bonneville Dam, farthest downstream in the Columbia River, forms a fifty-mile-long reservoir that reaches upstream to The Dalles Dam. Curving fish ladders by which salmon migrating to their spawning grounds can ascend from the river below the dam to the reservoir above it have been set up on both sides of the Columbia. A navigation lock permits boats and barges to pass.

Western Oregon covers no more than about a third of the state's 96,981 square miles, but it has nearly three-fourths of Oregon's total population. Their New England heritage has given the majority of Oregonians a conservative nature that frowns on highly speculative enterprises. Neither are they eager to encourage a concentration of industrial plants in their cities. They do not wish to have air or water pollution such as many other industrial cities have.

The region has a climate quite similar to that of western Washington with frequent rain from November to early May and summers in which there is little or no rain. Winter seldom brings snow to western Oregon and on the rare occasions that snow does fall in the Willamette valley it is such a wet snow that it melts almost instantly.

Eastern Oregon: Land of Contrasts

THE TOWNS of eastern Oregon sprang from cattle country "cow towns," gold-strike boom towns, and stagecoach stops. None of them is large, and some still have the appearance and atmosphere of the Old West. Pine-clad mountain ranges, sparkling blue lakes, and parched deserts form patterns of natural beauty in a vast lonely land. Oregon east of the crest of the Cascades has almost twice the area of western Oregon but only a small fraction of the state's total population.

This is a land of great contrasts. There are lonely deserts, lava plateaus, and vast mountain ranges. The Wallowa Mountains with beautiful Wallowa Lake in a niche among them occupy the northeastern corner of eastern Oregon. This was the land dear to the heart of Old Joseph, chief of the Nez Percé. When he was dying he begged his son, Young Joseph, to never let the Wallowa paradise fall into the hands of the white man. It was a perfect million-acre sanctuary that was well protected by the canyons of the Grande Ronde River on its western edge and by the Snake River which flows by Idaho's Seven Devils Mountains on the east. The Blue Mountains lapping over the Oregon border into southeastern Washington extend southward west of the Grande Ronde, then curve westward toward central Oregon and the distant Cascades. The Ochoco Mountains, rich in beds of fossilized prehistoric creatures, lie below the Blue Mountains. South of the Ochocos are the Harney High Lava Plains and the sagebrush and bunch grass of the Oregon Desert. Sparsely forested foothills and tule marshes cover the lake country of the southwest. Forests of ponderosa pine

Overlooking the Wallowa Mountains and Wallowa Lake in eastern Oregon

clothe the eastern slopes of the Cascades from Klamath Falls almost all the way to Hood River on the Columbia. The north central portion is dominated by the high plateau cut by the Deschutes River, a French name meaning "River of the Falls," and the John Day River.

Winters have always been cold in eastern Oregon. Heavy snowfalls and bitter cold spelled extreme hardship and disaster for many an exploring party that dared to enter this land during winter in the fur-trading era. When cattle and sheep were first brought to eastern Oregon, entire herds were sometimes buried beneath four to five feet of snow out on the grasslands.

The lush grasslands on the meadows of the high plateau through which the Deschutes River flowed caught the eye of cattlemen long before the first settlers came into the region. By the dawn of the present century big ranches had been built. A few covered one hundred thousand acres or more and had ten to twenty thousand head of cattle. Herds roamed freely to forage for themselves. Cowboys rode over the range to search for the cattle at roundup time when some were branded and others were taken in cattle drives to markets.

The arrival of settlers created a need for land to be used for growing crops. This led to the subdividing of some of the largest ranches. The era of the cattle baron who could make a fortune from beef cattle raised on the "free" grass of the open range was approaching an end. This way of ranching had often proved wasteful of both land and animals. Much of the grazing land used today is within the boundaries of national forests. Its use is controlled by permits issued by the Forest Service and limits the number of cattle that can graze in a given area. The purpose is to protect the shrubs and trees from overgrazing and insure enough space to provide for the animals' forage needs. Eastern Oregon forests are ideal for grazing since the dry climate eliminates a dense undergrowth of shrubs and vines such as that which luxuriates in a moist climate like that of western Oregon.

Sheep raisers came to eastern Oregon some years after the cattlemen. Basque immigrants, most of them sheepherders, whose homeland had been the Pyrénées of northwestern Spain, settled in the southeastern part of the state. A Basque loves life in a lonely land and the individual freedom it permits. They found the sagebrush and bunchgrass country of the upper Owyhee River valley and Rattlesnake Creek the kind of a land they liked.

Today Jordan City is a Basque town of only a couple of hundred inhabitants near the Oregon-Idaho state line and not far from the Jordan River, a tributary of the Owyhee. Its people live in houses built of stone with interiors decorated in bright colors. On festive occasions they don gaily colored folk costumes like those worn in their homeland and join, with the snapping of fingers, in dancing the fandango. Other folk dances like the vintage and weaving dances have been brought to the new land. Basque music and *pelota*, the national game which is much like our game of handball, are popular among the inhabitants. They have kept many of the old traditions and customs of the Basque provinces of Spain. Basque towns and sheepherders can

Idaho's famed Basque dancers provide colorful entertainment at community events throughout the state.

be found throughout the extreme southeastern part of Oregon westward from Jordan Valley toward Malheur Lake. Many Basques also live across the Oregon border in southwestern Idaho.

Ontario, Vale, Owyhee, Nyssa, and other small towns lie some one hundred miles north of Jordan Valley in a region that was once sagebrush and bunch-grass country. In recent decades the area has responded to the magic of water brought to its fields by irrigation canals. Ontario, the largest town in the area, is a trading center. The outlying fields grow sugar beets, onions, potatoes, and hay. Neighboring Nyssa has a large refinery using the sugar-beet crop as the source of the sugar.

Westward across Oregon's southeast corner is the town of Burns with a population of nearly four thousand, in the heart of a region of cattle ranches and lumber mills. In the vicinity are many areas of particular interest to hobbyists. Rock hounds search the hills and canyons for specimens of agates, jasper, thunder eggs, and fossils and are usually well rewarded for their efforts. Bird watchers and nature lovers in general have as much fun observing the water fowl that come from many parts of the continent to neighboring lakes during migrations. South of Malheur Lake is the Malheur National Wildlife Refuge which consists of 184,000 acres where many species of water fowl stop to rest and feed on their long spring or autumn migrations between their breeding grounds in the Canadian prairies and their winter homes in California or Mexico.

The Oregon Desert is lonely country, parched in summer and very cold in winter. Beef cattle graze on the sparse bunch grass. Antelope roam over the Steen Mountains, a range one hundred miles long, in the southeast. Near the western edge is the Hart Mountain National Antelope Refuge, a 240,000-acre sanctuary for the pronghorn antelope and the sage hen. During the migration seasons water fowl swarm in the lakes and tule marshes westward beyond the desert. Much of this desert country is in Harney County, Oregon's largest.

Baker, directly east of Elkhorn Ridge on Powder River, was the center of mining activity about one hundred years ago when gold was discovered in Griffin's Gulch. A rash of boom towns sprang up in the surrounding country at that time. Baker became the trading center through which freight wagons and stagecoaches passed. Today it thrives on the trade from cattle ranches, farms, and the lumber industry. Many of the old boom towns became ghost towns when gold could no longer be found in mountain streams. A few still stand like Bonanza, Greenhorn, McEwen, and Cornucopia; most of them mere empty shells with perhaps a few old-timers whiling away the hours.

One of the most widely known towns of the area is Pendleton, built on a plateau above the north bank of the Umatilla River. Hills rise abruptly behind the town. Around it are many square miles of wheat fields which reach toward the Columbia and the Blue Mountains. There are woolen, flour, and lumber mills in Pendleton. In mid-September banners bearing the slogan "Let 'er Buck" span the streets. False building fronts representing the hotels, saloons, banks, and stores of the Old West are set up; and the stadium is packed to capacity with crowds who come to watch the bronco riding, steer roping, and other western activities. This is the time of the Roundup, an annual celebration in Pendleton since 1910. Umatilla Indians in their finest robes, buckskin shirts resplendent with beadwork and elk's teeth, and war bonnets bristling with eagle feathers, mingle with the crowds on Pendleton's streets and take part in the Westward Ho Parade. Spur chains jingle as cowboys wearing Stetson hats strut down the main streets. There are squaws with papooses cradled on their backs, old stagecoaches drawn by teams of horses, and oxen yoked to prairie schooners.

West along the Columbia there are several very small towns. The Dalles and Hood River are the largest. The Dalles began long before the first covered wagons came over the Oregon Trail. Emigrants halted at The Dalles to embark on bateaus or rafts for the voyage down the rapids to Fort Vancouver. Today the rapids are gone. The long lake behind the dam has taken their place. Ocean vessels that use the navigation locks of the downstream dams often moor at The Dalles to load cargo. Hood River is in one of the finest apple-growing regions of the Pacific Northwest. In spring the valley is a sea of pink blossoms with the white cone of Mount Hood looming above it.

Farther south along the western edge of the region are fields of potatoes and grain in the Crooked River country. The towns of Redmond and Prineville, both farm-trading centers, have mills which cut timber logged in the nearby forests of pine into lumber. The town of Madras is well known for the precious stones that can be found in the surrounding region.

Bend and Klamath Falls, the largest towns in the pine-clad foothills of the Cascades, are gateways to areas where deer are plentiful and lakes and mountain streams are well-stocked with trout. Skiers come to Bend to reach the Hoodoo Bowl in Santiam Pass in the Cascades. Southeast of Bend there are lava formations and several ice caves that attract those interested in such geological formations. The entire region is grazing country for beef cattle.

Klamath Falls is the larger of the two towns and lies below the southern tip of Upper Klamath Lake, fifty miles long with several wildlife refuges along its shores. The white pelican nests along this and other nearby lakes. Loggers, cattlemen from outlying ranches, and Indians from the Klamath Reservation make Klamath Falls, a town of about 17,000 inhabitants, their trading center.

There is no manufacturing in eastern Oregon. Its population is small, a mere fraction of that of western Oregon. Agriculture, sheep raising, and lumber are the major interests. Summers in eastern Oregon are hot and dry and the lack of rain there has created desert conditions in the southeastern and south-central areas of the region. More than one fourth of eastern Oregon is barren wasteland of value only as grazing country.

Idaho: Land of Sun Coming Down the Mountains

CAPTAIN MERIWETHER LEWIS and two companions crossed the Continental Divide by way of Lemhi Pass through the Bitterroot Range of the Rockies on August 12, 1805. It was a memorable event in American history. At last a way had been found through the great mountain barrier to exploration of the unknown country that lay westward to the ocean. In the journal he kept of the expedition Lewis wrote of proceeding to the top of the dividing ridge. Looking west he saw more ranges of high mountains, their peaks partially covered with snow. Less than a mile down the steep western slope was a creek flowing clear and cold, eventually to the Columbia. The three men entered a land of rugged mountains, wild raging streams, and sparkling lakes formed from the meltwater of snow fields and glaciers. They had entered the future state of Idaho. It is said that the name Idaho in the language of the Shoshoni Indians means "Look! The sun coming down the mountains."

Idaho's 83,557 square miles is roughly ten times the area of Massachusetts but it has no more than one eighth of the population of that New England state. Where the tip of the Idaho panhandle borders Canada, it is only forty-five miles wide. Along the state's southern border which touches Nevada and Utah its width is 305 miles. Idaho is bordered to the west by Oregon and Washington and this part of the state includes a 200-mile stretch of the Snake River with deep Hell's Canyon just west of Seven Devils Mountains. Part of the eastern border is the Continental Divide where waters draining from the western slopes

The Sawtooth Mountains, one of Idaho's spectacular mountain ranges, with Sun Valley in the foreground

flow to the Pacific; waters from the eastern slope, to the Atlantic. Mount Borah (12,662 ft.), Idaho's highest peak, is in the Sawtooth Mountains. It was named for Senator William E. Borah who served as United States senator from Idaho from 1907–1940.

The Idaho panhandle is a forested region which includes one fourth of the total area of the state. It has many mountain ranges, including the Bitterroot, Coeur d'Alene, Clearwater, and Cabinet ranges, with peaks of six to eight thousand feet or more in height. Today it is a land of sawmills, mines, and forests where bear, elk, moose, and deer make their home. There are a few plateaus in the west where much of the land is devoted to agriculture. Veins of silver, lead, and zinc ores are buried in the mountains. Gold is also found. More than a century ago fine grains of gold were found in the soil underlying the sod of an alpine meadow near Pierce, the first discovery of gold in Idaho. News of this gold strike brought prospectors swarming into the diggings. Silver discovered near Coeur d'Alene in 1884 prompted another stampede of men eager to make a fortune in a hurry.

When breezes sweep through the northern panhandle's forests they whisper among the branches of yellow, white, and lodgepole pines, giant cedars, and other cone-bearing trees. The lodgepole pine got its name from the use the Indians made of its tall slender trunk, which they used as poles for their lodges or teepees. Some of the finest timber was cut half a century ago by loggers. Second growth timber supplies some of the trees for the lumber industry today. Cutting in virgin forests in much of Idaho is under strict control and reforestation is providing for future needs. Eight-hundred-thousand-acre Coeur d'Alene National Forest has some of the finest stands of white pine despite a costly fire that wiped out a large part of it many years ago.

A stiff breeze in the region sometimes sends waves thirty feet high rolling across Lake Pend Oreille, the largest lake in the state. It lies in the Cabinet Mountains, fed by the cascading waters of Clark Fork River. Its outlet, at its northwestern tip, is the Pend Oreille River which flows across the border into Washington. Islands near its western shore were once the cemeteries of Indians who hung the bodies of their dead from the branches of trees instead of burying them. Cedar lumber is shipped from the town of Sandpoint on the lake's north shore.

French-Canadian trappers and traders combed much of the northern part of Idaho in the early days and bartered for beaver pelts. From them we get such names as Pend Oreille and Coeur d'Alene. Pend Oreille is the name the French-Canadians gave a tribe of Indians, many of whom wore shell earrings. Pend Oreille means "earring." Coeur d'Alene means "pointed or awl heart." The Indians had "hearts like awls" according to these traders because they would not take mere trinkets in exchange for their beaver pelts. They demanded something of real value for them. Many other place names are also of French-Canadian origin.

Lake Coeur d'Alene is twenty-two miles long. It lies in the heart of the white-pine country. Coeur d'Alene and St. Joe rivers, both of which have their source in the Bitterroot Range, flow into the lake. Mills where white pine is cut into lumber are in the lakeside town of Coeur d'Alene. In the vicinity are large orchards of plum trees.

Throughout mountainous eastern Idaho in this part of the panhandle boom towns sprang up overnight when news of a gold or silver strike got around. Some grew to be towns with several thousand inhabitants. When the pay dirt gave out miners went to other regions where new strikes had been made. Cabins, stables, hotels, stores, and mines were deserted and most boom towns became ghost towns. A few survived, however, and when more effective mining equipment arrived they grew larger and prospered. Wallace and Kellogg were among the survivors and they continue to operate and grow today. The Sunshine Mine, largest silver mine in the United States, is in Kellogg; the Bunker Hill Mine, two miles away, has its smelters extracting lead from the rich deposits of lead-zinc ore in nearby mountains. Several other mines producing silver, lead, and zinc are in the area.

The Mission of the Sacred Heart was begun in 1847 by Father Ravalli on a site between Coeur d'Alene and Kellogg. Indians helped in constructing the mission. It was completed twenty years later. Father Ravalli taught the Indians Christianity and agriculture as well. The mission was reconstructed in recent years to help recall the early days of Idaho. Paintings done by Indians with the dyes they made hang on the walls of its chapel.

South of Wallace in the eastern part of the panhandle there are no large towns. The greater part of the region has been set aside as the Selway-Bitterroot Wilderness Area where modern developments are restricted to preserve the natural beauty of the area and to protect its wildlife.

The towns of Moscow and Lewiston, in a region of farms, orchards and grain fields, are near the Idaho-Washington border. Field peas is a major crop in the Palouse valley around Moscow. This town is also the seat of the University of Idaho.

The famous Primitive Area of central Idaho has more than a million acres of unspoiled mountains, forests, and canyons within its borders. No roads cross the area; exploration must be made by foot or by pack horse. Most of the region lies south of the Salmon River and includes a number of national forests with large stands of yellow pine, fir, and lodgepole pine. It is the home of thousands of mule deer and hundreds of elk and bear. Pictographs found on the walls of caves prove that thousands of years ago primitive man roamed through its valleys and canyons. Roads will never be built to its most beautiful waterfalls, lakes, and gorges. Nothing will be permitted to mar the beauty of the region. A few small isolated ranches and mines are in the area. Planes carry big-game hunters and adventurous sightseers to some of its canyons and alpine meadows. Trails that penetrate this wilderness will eventually be extended. The number who visit the Primitive Area has increased enormously in the last few years. The Salmon River which Lewis judged too hazardous for travel by canoe to the Columbia is now a source of breath-taking adventure. Inflated rubber rafts and boats are used to descend the raging waters today. Where the canoes of the Lewis and Clark expedition would have been

Salmon River, once known as the "River of No Return," flows through White Bird Canyon, an area rich in history.

splintered or crushed along the tortuous course these inflated rubber craft bounce away from the boulders and rock walls they strike. The Salmon River is no longer the "River of No Return." The Indians gave it that name because the strength of its current prevents return upstream by canoe. Today's jet boats have solved the problem of the return trip. They carry thrill-seeking passengers safely back up the river's canyons.

Idaho is rich in history. The Nez Percé National Historical Park in the central part of the state includes twenty-two sites under the care of the National Park Service. Nearly all are related in some way by historical events associated with the Nez Percé Indians or with their culture. One, near Lewiston, is the site of Lapwai mission, begun in 1836, where the missionaries Henry and Eliza Spalding worked with the Nez Percé. The buildings were destroyed during an attack by a hostile band of Indians following the massacre of the Whitmans at their mission near Walla Walla in Washington. The Lapwai mission was abandoned in 1847. Another site is the battlefield beside the little village of White Bird where Indians under the command of Chief Joseph defeated United States cavalry units in a brilliant military maneuver. Clearwater Battlefield and Canoe Camp on the Clearwater River where the Lewis and Clark expedition built dugouts for their trip down the Columbia in 1805 are sites in the park. The Weis Rockshelter in Grave Creek Canyon which reveals evidence that prehistoric people lived there eight thousand years ago is another place of interest in the park.

Many horses are raised in Idaho where they are still very useful animals. Modern farm equipment has taken over much of the work in the fields formerly done with horses, but for herding cattle in the sage-brush and dry grass country and climbing steep-sloped hills there is no substitute for the horse. On cattle ranches and at mountain and lake resorts the horse fills a definite need. In some isolated parts of the state wild horses still roam at will.

Two very popular recreation centers on the edge of southern Idaho are Payette Lake and Sun Valley. Skiing, bobsledding, and ice-skating draw thousands who are interested in winter sports to Sun Valley Lodge and the neighboring town of Ketchum below the thirty-mile-long Sawtooth Range. It is an area famous for winter fun. At the edge of the forest skirting the shore of Payette Lake, the little town of McCall boasts fine skiing all year. In winter skiers take to the powder snow on nearby slopes. In summer there is no snow, but plenty of water-skiing on the lake. The Sawtooth Mountains north of Sun Valley have more than forty peaks that rise to altitudes of ten thousand feet or more and about two hundred beautiful lakes, including popular Redfish Lake.

Emigrant wagon trains creaked across southern Idaho in the forties and fifties of the last century. It was a thirsty sagebrush country, an uninviting land devoid of trees. Ruts of the Oregon Trail can still be found where those wagon trains hugged the hills north of the Snake. A rest stop was made at Fort Hall and again at Fort Boise both of which offered welcome relief from the dust and the rigors of travel.

Old Fort Hall is merely a memory now. The cabins, stores, stables, and blockhouse built by the Yankee trader, Nathaniel Wyeth, in 1834 were sold to Hudson's Bay in 1838. Then, long after fur traders departed from the region, the fort continued to serve as a station for emigrants traveling on the Oregon Trail. In 1855 it was abandoned, but for several years more it still stood on the site where it had been an island of safety while battles between warriors of the Blackfoot and Bannock tribes swirled around it. Eventually floods ate into the adobe covering of the stockade and the walls of its buildings until gradually all of the skeleton that remained was washed away. The site of the fort is now on an Indian reservation near the town of Fort Hall.

Water worked like magic in transforming Idaho's dry sagebrush country into lush green fields of potatoes, beans, and alfalfa, with apple orchards and acres of sugar beets stretching toward the horizon. The first use of irrigation in the state was made at Franklin, a Mormon settlement, in 1860. A ditch was dug to carry the water from a nearby creek to the fields beyond. Now more than five thousand diversion dams and almost four hundred reservoirs serve the farmers of Idaho. Many thousands of miles of canals form a network that brings water from rivers, lakes, springs, and wells. Tracts of many thousands of acres of thirsty land still wait for the day when the magic of water will convert them to productive fields.

The biggest source of water is the Snake River and the largest plots of farmland are in its valley and on its plain. The Snake rises from three small lakes in Yellowstone Park across the Wyoming border. Then it flows south to broaden and form crystal clear Jackson Lake in the Teton country, a beaver-rich land which was once the rendezvous of traders. The Snake River follows a long canyon from Teton Valley in Wyoming to emerge near the town of Idaho Falls. Around this town of nearly thirty-six thousand inhabitants water flows through irrigation canals to the fields of Idaho russet potatoes. Huge shipments from this and other parts of southern Idaho make the state rank first in the nation as a producer of potatoes. Culls not suitable for marketing bring additional income when they are converted to potato flour and starch.

On a high desert land west of Idaho Falls not far from the Craters of the Moon National Monument is Arco where the reactors of the National Reactor Testing Station of the Atomic Energy Commission are being used to develop peaceful uses of atomic energy. Electricity produced from the atom is being used to provide light and power for Arco.

Pocatello is slightly bigger than Idaho Falls. It is the second largest city in the state and a major railroad center. Southwest of Pocatello the Portneuf River, a small tributary of the Snake, flows from the mountains of Caribou County. This and neighboring Bear County are in a beaver-rich region. Most of the towns of the region originated as settlements of Mormons who trekked north from Utah in early times. Malad City, with about two thousand inhabitants, is one of the interesting towns of southeastern Idaho. Its past is steeped in stories of lynchings, stagecoach holdups, and the robbing of wagons that brought gold from the mines of northern Idaho and Montana through the town on their way to Utah smelters. Its crooked streets and old buildings make it easy to picture these happenings of almost a century ago. North of Pocatello is Fort Hall and, west of it, Burley, with more potato flour mills in another potato-growing region that also is known for its big crops of beans, onions, and fruit.

The lush farmland region from American Falls to Twin Falls along the Snake River is known as the Magic Valley. Water needs for its farmlands come from an annual rainfall of between eight to ten inches plus whatever irrigation is necessary.

Idaho's southwest corner, the Owyhee country, is barren desert where sagebrush and greasewood grow. In its northern part ghost towns are monuments to more prosperous days when purchases were made with gold dust panned from creeks in the mountains. Beef cattle or sheep graze where bunch grass thrives. Black basalt bluffs loom ominously above tawny drifts of sand which are heaped high with drifts of snow shifted by winter winds. The Snake River has cut deep gorges in the land and the Bruneau River has carved canyons so narrow a stone can be thrown from rim to rim and so deep in places sunlight cannot reach its foaming waters one thousand feet or more below. Coyotes howl at night in this lonely Owyhee country; horned toads and rattlesnakes seek shelter from the midday sun.

Silver City is one of the best preserved of the Owyhee ghost towns. It mushroomed in the mountains when gold was found in Jordan Creek in 1863 and became a city so prosperous its townsfolk boasted that trade and people would be drawn from Boise to Silver City. Several thousand lived there then. A recent check of its population found seven old-timers living amid the ruins of what once were swank hotels, stores, and homes, abandoned when the gold gave out.

Boise is Idaho's largest city with more than 60,000 people and the capital of the state. The capitol in the heart of the business district looks down the main street toward the beautiful Spanish-style Union Pacific Railway station across the Boise River. Some of Boise's homes are heated by hot water from natural wells and springs near the city as are some other homes in cities in southern Idaho. The city has many fine parks. A number of buildings that were built during the pioneer era have been brought to Julia Davis Park from various parts of the state. Around the city there are farms and a number of small towns including Nampa, Caldwell, Emmett, Payette, and Weiser.

From the town of Adrian, across the border in Oregon, the Snake River forms the boundary between Oregon and Idaho as far north as Lewiston where it is joined by the Clearwater River. Here it turns west to flow across southeastern Washington to its juncture with the Columbia near Pasco. There are several canyons in the lower part of the Snake. The most spectacular and deepest is Hell's Canyon which parallels Seven Devils Mountains. This canyon averages four to nine miles wide and is well over a mile deep. It will be merely a memory several years from now when a high dam is built to make the canyon a reservoir for irrigation and the generating of hydroelectric power.

For years the lack of irrigation and the small amount of rainfall left many parts of southern Idaho dry and unproductive. The construction of dams for irrigation in the Snake River and many of its tributaries has eliminated much of this problem. Thousands of acres of farmland have replaced much of the barren wasteland of that area.

Although grazing has been restricted in Idaho, sheep raising is still an important industry.

The population of Idaho is small and local demand for the produce of its farms is not large. However, most of the large towns are on transcontinental railroad lines and highways which give easy access to distant markets. Only about one third of the land in Idaho is privately owned; about three fourths has been set aside as national forests, primitive areas, or other state or federal lands. This of course places restrictions on the cutting of timber and grazing. The limitations on grazing in national forests and the breaking up of large ranches to provide farms has reduced cattle and sheep production to some extent.

Roads are costly in the panhandle of Idaho because the high mountain ranges run in a north to south direction with deep canyons to be spanned by bridges. Because of this lumbering and mining are the major industries. It is believed there is an abundance of silver deposits in the panhandle that have never been tapped. Hydroelectric power and water are both plentiful in the north and can lead to the establishing of electrochemical industries.

British Columbia: Land of Mountains

BRITISH COLUMBIA is a land of many contrasts. Some areas on Vancouver Island's west coast have an annual rainfall of more than two hundred and fifty inches while in sagebrush and bunch-grass country not far from Kamloops on the mainland the sun shines most of the year and the annual rainfall is seldom more than eight inches. Small communities of the interior of the province have many of the characteristics of the frontier town of fifty or a hundred years ago while Vancouver, the largest city of the province, has freeways, high-rise apartment houses, and traffic snarls. In December roses bloom in the gardens of Victoria homes on the southern tip of Vancouver Island at the same time that snow crunches underfoot in Prince George at a temperature of forty degrees below freezing.

This is a big province, covering 366,255 square miles, almost one and a half times the size of Idaho, Oregon, and Washington combined. Most of its 1,838,000 inhabitants live in a relatively narrow zone near the American border; 828,000 of these live in the greater Vancouver area alone. The entire province stretches from the forty-ninth to the sixtieth parallel, more than eight hundred miles in length and from the Pacific to the crest of the Rockies, more than four hundred miles in width. Its central part is a high plateau freckled with hundreds of lakes teeming with trout. So great is the number of snow-capped peaks in its sea of mountains that there are many that have not yet been named. A mesh of small swiftly flowing streams carry the meltwater of mountain glaciers and snow fields to the Fraser and the

Columbia and their tributaries. Clusters of islands off the coast frame a well-traveled, well-protected waterway that reaches from the Strait of Juan de Fuca to southeastern Alaska, the whole length of the province. The largest is Vancouver Island in the south, almost three hundred miles long. The big Queen Charlotte group, steeped in the lore of the Haida Indians, is well offshore in the north. Between these and the fringe of islands along the shore of the mainland are the Strait of Georgia, Johnstone Strait, Queen Charlotte Strait, Queen Charlotte Sound, which becomes rough when storms whip up the waters of the open sea, and Hecata Strait. These form what is known as the "Inside Passage," used by coastal ships to avoid the turbulent Pacific.

Settlers came late to this part of the Pacific Northwest. This was fur traders' land, and the big British companies hoped to keep it that way. In 1843, Hudson's Bay's western headquarters were transferred from Fort Vancouver to Fort Victoria on Vancouver Island. James Douglas, who began as a fur trader, had become the company's head man in the northwest. In 1849 one of the first shiploads of colonists arrived from England at the new post and in 1850 Vancouver Island became a British colony. Douglas was made governor of the colony of Vancouver Island. The discovery of coal near Nanaimo north of Victoria brought a few more settlers. Then a discovery that was to bring great changes to the colony was made in 1858. Gold was found in the sand and gravel of the bed of the Fraser River near Hope on the mainland. Miners rushed to the scene. Many came from California by way of Bellingham south of the border. Others came by the hundreds aboard ships to Victoria. Soon discoveries of gold were made at Yale, farther up the Fraser; then in the region of the Quesnel River and the Cariboo Hills. More men came to pan or dig for gold. Barkerville became a boom town in the Cariboo district. In this area an attempt was made to use camels as a means of transporting freight to the mines. The animals were purchased from the United States Army which had tried to use them as pack animals in the desert country of the American southwest without success. They also proved unsatisfactory along the narrow canyon-wall trails of the Fraser but for a different reason. Complaints from mule-train drivers put an end to this experiment; the sight of the camels so thoroughly frightened the mules on those narrow tortuous trails that such meetings usually ended in disaster.

No legal government existed on the mainland when the gold rush to the Fraser began since the British government had not established a colony there. Governor Douglas, however, took control. Shortly after news of the gold strike reached London, the Crown Colony of British

Columbia was created, and Douglas was appointed the new colony's first governor in 1858. This added greatly to the responsibilities of Governor Douglas. He was now the head of two separate colonies. Two years later the two were merged to form one colony—the Colony of British Columbia with the capital in Victoria. In 1871 the Colony of British Columbia became a province of the Dominion of Canada after the Dominion government in Ottawa promised that a railroad would be built across the Rockies to the Pacific to link British Columbia with the provinces to the east.

Vancouver Island has a rugged mountain backbone clothed with a luxuriant growth of tall Douglas fir, hemlock, and red cedar. Some of the mountains rise to heights of ten thousand feet. Lakes are set in the narrow valleys between the mountain ridges which run parallel to the island's shore. This has made road construction to the west coast of the island costly and difficult. Only on the opposite side, facing the straits and the mainland, is there a wide stretch of fairly level land suitable for farming. Small fishing villages reached only by boat or seaplane are strung along the west coast. Here also are long fingerlike, dead-end channels poking into the mountains. One of the largest is forty miles long. It reaches to Port Alberni with its lumber, plywood, and pulp mills and fishing fleet moorings. Port Renfrew, Clo-oose, Tofino, Nootka, and Port Alice are small towns facing the Pacific on Vancouver Island's west coast. Nootka is at the entrance to the sound where ships of early explorers dropped anchor in Friendly Cove.

Victoria, the provincial capital at the southern tip of the island, has a very mild climate, ideal for the growing of many kinds of shrubs and flowers. Along streets skirting the sea, shaded by sprawling oaks, there are homes in the English style set among beautiful gardens. Holly is grown commercially on small farms in this part of the island for the Christmas season. In early spring daffodils are harvested for shipment to cities of the prairie provinces and eastern Canada for the Easter trade. Flanking the Inner Harbor in downtown Victoria are the gray-stone Parliament Building and the famous vine-clad Empress Hotel where traditional English Yuletide celebrations are held each year.

Farther north on the east shore of the island is Nanaimo whose major interests today are lumber and fish. Campbell River, a few miles north, is the site of paper and pulp mills. One of the major difficulties to be faced in the further development of Vancouver Island is the lack of roads to the west coast. Much of the freight brought to island towns in the west from mainland terminals in Vancouver comes in boxcars

Fishing in British Columbia waters

loaded on barges towed by tugs or on the ferries which shuttle between the island and the mainland.

Transportation can be a problem on the mainland too. Much of the mainland coast north of Bliss Landing has no connection with the rest of the province other than by boat or plane. There are no highways or railroads along the coast. The major northern towns—such as Kitimat and Prince Rupert—do have highways leading to the interior.

Kitimat was built by the company that constructed one of the world's largest aluminum smelters nearby. The town is at the head of eighty-mile-long Douglas Channel that leads inland from Hecata Strait and is deep enough to permit ocean vessels to bring the bauxite ore from which aluminum is extracted which they get from the island of Jamaica in the West Indies right up to the Kitimat docks. This channel and the hydroelectric power from a plant built inside a nearby mountain

Vessels of the British Columbia fishing fleet

at Kemano have made it feasible to have the smelter at Kitimat. Water which flows through the turbines generating the electricity necessary to the process comes from a 358-square-mile lake or reservoir created in the mountains of the Coast Range by the construction of the Kenny Dam. Aluminum transmission lines carry the current more than fifty miles across forests, canyons, inlets, and mountain ridges to the Kitimat smelter.

British Columbia's coastal waters provide the harvest upon which the fishing industry of the province depends. Salmon constitute a major share of the industry with sockeye and spring salmon the most prized species. The Fraser and the Skeena rivers are the best sockeye streams on the entire Pacific coast. Canneries which receive the catch are located in Prince Rupert and Vancouver. Halibut, sole, cod, shrimp, and herring are also caught.

Beyond the dense forests, coastal Indian villages, and peaks and glaciers of the Coast Range, lies the cattle, grain, and fruit country of the rolling inland plateau. The Fraser cuts diagonally across it from Prince George to Lytton near its juncture with the Thompson River. A sawmill and railroad town, Prince George is on the threshold of the heart of British Columbia where the northern part of the province begins. The Chilcotin region of grasslands and stands of pine and spruce is west of the Fraser; the Cariboo district is east of it. Chilcotin ranches average about three thousand acres. A few are much larger. Cattle graze in the area during the summer and are then driven to the lower Fraser valley for winter feeding. The Cariboo was once gold country where fortunes were made almost overnight. In the 1860s many lives were lost there, and crime was rampant.

At that time Barkerville was a distributing center for miners' supplies. Today it lives on its historic past. Visitors swarm to this ghost town during the summer. When mining activity slowed, cattle that had been brought in as a supply of beef for the miners were taken over by ranches and this started the cattle industry of the region. Today Williams Lake, not far from Barkerville, is a trading center for cattlemen of the area.

Northwest of the Chilcotin region is Tweedsmuir Provincial Park, a wilderness mountain and lake region. The lakes are long and narrow, some with an area of ninety to one hundred square miles. This is a lonely beautiful land with practically no roads except the one main highway from Vanderhoof to Smithers. Just north of Vanderhoof amid more lakes is Fort St. James in the country which Simon Fraser named New Caledonia. There is no farming in this region since morning frost occurs during most of the year.

The rapids of the Fraser, which made travel by canoe extremely hazardous, end at Lytton. The most dangerous section, Hells Gate Canyon near the town of Boston Bar, is the narrow rock-walled stretch which claimed the lives of so many who dared to venture through it by canoe. Sockeye salmon have always fought their way upstream against these rapids. In 1913 a rockslide during construction of the railroad through the canyon almost completely blocked the route for salmon. The Fraser's reputation as one of the great salmon streams of the northwest was at stake. Fish ladders were built. Now the number of fish successful in reaching spawning grounds above the canyon has resulted in runs even greater than before. The Shuswap Indians live in this part of British Columbia. Their favorite fishing station to which they come each summer is the juncture of the Thompson and the Fraser. At Hope the river leaves the narrow valley it follows between the Lilloet and Cascade ranges and turns west into a wide fertile valley of dairy farms. It passes Chilliwack and New Westminster on its way to Vancouver where it spills out into the Strait of Georgia. Fort Langley in the lower valley, once the provisional capital of the province, has been reconstructed to appear as it did in the days when Governor Douglas took control of the region.

Several long narrow lakes shimmer in the sunshine which floods much of the southern part of the province between the Cascades and Monashee mountains most of the year. Lake Okanagan reaches from Penticton, a town bordered on two sides by fine lakeside beaches, to some distance beyond Vernon. The town of Kelowna lies midway between them. It is a striking example of a community that has not sacrificed natural beauty for industry. On the edge of its business district is a well-groomed park bordering a wide sandy beach. Each summer a regatta is held that attracts hundreds of visitors. Partly submerged a few feet offshore is Ogopogo, a brightly colored replica of the mythical serpent which is said to live in the lake.

The Okanagan country receives less than fifteen inches of rainfall a year, but irrigation provides enough for the growing of crops. Its peach, apricot, apple, pear, and cherry orchards have made the Okanagan valley the fruit bowl of British Columbia. The fruit packing is done in Vernon and Kelowna. Dairy cattle graze in the meadows of the valley and some grain is harvested.

Farther north around Kamloops and Ashcroft there are cattle ranches. Revelstoke, a small town to the east of these on the Columbia River, nestles below Mount Revelstoke which has been set aside as a provincial park. A few miles away are Glacier National Park, the village of Golden, and Yoho National Park. In a mountain near Kicking Horse Pass is the unusual spiral tunnel of the transcontinental railroad line over the Rockies. When a long freight train travels through this tunnel, the locomotive can be seen from the highway emerging from the tunnel while the caboose has not yet entered it.

The Columbia River flows north through Golden to Boat Encampment on the route Mackenzie took in winter at temperatures far below zero. Boat Encampment, which became a station on the route of the Hudson's Bay Company's canoe brigades, will be flooded when dams that are to be built are completed on the upper Columbia. Farther north another provincial park includes Mount Robson, the highest peak in the Canadian Rockies, with an altitude of 12,972 feet, and its Valley of a Thousand Falls. Throughout this mountainous region along the eastern edge of the province it is possible to see bighorn sheep and mountain goats climbing the bleak rocky ramparts of alpine ridges,

Kicking Horse Pass in Yoho National Park provides a scenic passage through the Rockies for the transcontinental railroad and highway.

moose wading in marshlands to feed on succulent roots and stems, and birds of prey circling high above forests of lodgepole pine.

Between the several ranges of the Monashee and Purcell mountains in southeastern British Columbia are Upper and Lower Arrow lakes. They are actually a widening of the Columbia on its way south. At one time paddle-wheel steamers carried passengers and freight on these and the lakes of the Okanagan country to the west. This is the Kootenay country where fortunes in gold, silver, copper, lead, and zinc have been reaped from the mountain ranges over the years. Near the southern tip of Lower Arrow Lake are the towns of Castlegar, Rossland, Trail, and Nelson. They all began as mining centers. Trail was built on the flood plain where Trail Creek joins the Columbia and its first smelter was constructed in 1896 to extract gold from its ores. Some gold is still extracted at Trail, but of greater importance there today is the lead and zinc taken from ores mined farther north. The fumes from the smelter, once a harmful nuisance to farmers across the border in the United States, now yield a very valuable by-product in the form of commercial fertilizers and insecticides.

British Columbia is a huge province with vast wealth in natural resources. Its hydroelectric power potential is enormous. Fish and game are plentiful. Minerals still lie hidden in untouched pockets yet to be discovered. To open mines, develop new areas, and locate and construct industrial facilities north of the southern zone where most of its population is concentrated is understandably costly for the province. Road building and railroad construction across its sea of high mountain ranges is slow and expensive. The province has done well in spite of its handicaps. For the industrial development of some of its potentially valuable resources it has relied on foreign capital. American companies have provided much. Swedish, Japanese, German, and British sources have also invested in the development of industrial projects in the province.

The people of British Columbia are aware of the wisdom of guarding the province's great wilderness areas, preserving its natural beauty, and protecting its watersheds and magnificent forests. Only a few large manufacturers have built plants in the region. British Columbia's big industries are paper, lumber, fisheries products, minerals, and export trade to the Far East, Australia, and New Zealand. Local demand is not great because the population is small and also because some local needs are satisfied by importing products from other lands, usually from Pacific Coast regions south of the Canadian border. Tourism, another major industry of the province today, will increase greatly as more roads are built to give access to areas of magnificent scenery not easily reached now.

The Big Cities: Seattle, Portland, and Vancouver

WHEN A STEAM MILL was built in the 1850s on its river front and oxen began dragging logs to be cut into lumber down some of its streets, the little village of Portland began to grow. It thrived on the trade which brought schooners up the Willamette to load the lumber needed in California. Two years after the founding of Alki in 1851, Henry Yesler built a sawmill on the water on the northeastern shore of Elliott Bay. The forest was cleared from the hills surrounding the little cluster of frame buildings that sprang up around the mill and Seattle became a busy town on Puget Sound. In 1867 an erstwhile seaman built a hotel among a cluster of shacks near a sawmill on the shore of Burrard Inlet. He was a man who loved to talk and tell tall tales and was generally known as Gassy Jack. The settlement went by the name of Gastown until it was changed to Granville and then, when the tracks of the transcontinental railroad reached it, it was finally changed to Vancouver. These grew to become the Pacific Northwest's three major cities.

Each of these cities is a major world port with well-protected harbors far inland from the coast. It is a gala event on the Vancouver waterfront when a huge liner glides under the Lions Gate Bridge at the harbor entrance and tugboats maneuver to bring her to her berth. Lumber and wheat go into the holds of freighters moored at the docks along the Willamette, Portland's fresh-water harbor. In Seattle, at piers fringing Alaskan Way and at those in Smith's Cove, longshoremen move cargo aboard ships from the Orient, Europe, California, and Alaska.

The three waterfront towns of slightly more than a century ago have grown far beyond the dreams of pioneer settlers. Today Seattle and Portland are major units in a chain nearly five hundred miles long of cities and towns that extends from the Canadian border to the college towns of Corvallis and Eugene in Oregon. Experts who study population trends predict all will eventually merge to form one huge megalopolis. "Pugetopolis" is a name already on the lips of leaders who envision an expanded Puget Sound area in the very near future and worry about the problems such expansion will bring. Seattle, largest of the three big cities, is about 160 miles north of Portland, the smallest and oldest of the three. The distance from Seattle to Vancouver across the Canadian border is about the same.

Seattle is shaped like an hourglass with its tallest buildings very near the middle. Its limits to the west are the shores of Puget Sound. In the near distance wooded islands, Kitsap Peninsula, and the long line of snow-crested peaks of the Olympic Range form a dramatic backdrop. At sunup these white ramparts become pink in the morning light, a sight every Seattleite views with great pride. To the east the city skirts the shore of twenty-six-mile-long Lake Washington. The peaks of the Cascade Range lie beyond with the highest, Mount Rainier, looming big on the horizon to the southeast. Floating bridges built on concrete pontoons span Lake Washington to link Seattle with Kirkland, Bellevue, and other towns on the opposite shore.

In the northern half of the hourglass are Lake Union rimmed by small manufacturing plants and, above it, Green Lake, on the edge of Woodland Park. Here also are residential areas and the campus of the University of Washington. The southern half of the hourglass includes the industrial district flanked on one side by the heights of West Seattle and on the other by Beacon Hill and Rainier Valley. Shipbuilding and ship repair are centered in the drydocks on man-made Harbor Island. Farther south, at the base of the hourglass, sprawls the Boeing Company's main plant. This aviation giant began as a small plant on Lake Union in 1917. Today its Seattle and nearby Renton plants turn out one airplane every day. This is Seattle's biggest industry. The city prospers when the Boeing payroll is high, and slows down when the backlog of airplane orders has dwindled and men are laid off work. Other manufacturing industries in Seattle are dwarfed by Boeing and the city is often branded a one-industry city with its economy highly sensitive to the fortunes of the Boeing Company.

Today near the site of Yesler's mill the totem pole in Pioneer Square faces building fronts that were constructed in the eighties and

Seattle's biggest industry. The Boeing Company's plants in Seattle and nearby Renton turn out airplanes at the rate of one every day.

nineties. Alki, now a residential area of Seattle, has beachside homes, beautiful rock gardens, a lighthouse on the point, and a popular salt-water bathing beach. Pioneer Square borders a district of cheap hotels, cabarets, and second-hand shops commonly called the "Skidroad." One of the largest international sections in the Pacific Northwest, known as Chinatown, lies beyond the railroad depots, not far from Pioneer Square. Its streets are lined with the shops of Chinese, Japanese, and Filipino merchants, Oriental cafés, and here and there a Buddhist temple. In its markets can be purchased bamboo shoots, fish cakes, sea-weed, and many other Oriental foods. The tall buildings near Pioneer

Square are in the financial district. A block away is the city's first sky-scraper, the Smith Tower, built in 1914. It reaches forty-two stories above street level and is architecturally a little out of place among its newer neighbors.

Not many years ago cable cars rattled and clanged on Madison and James streets. A third cable line carried passengers along Yesler Way, the hillside street that was once the skidroad to Yesler's mill. These lines served shoppers and office workers living on First Hill, Capitol Hill, and all points as far as Leschi Park on the shore of Lake Washington. Seattle, unlike San Francisco, ripped out her cable lines when her transit system was converted to trackless trolleys. The mono-rail came with Century '21, the World's Fair of 1962. Today its sleek streamlined cars whisk passengers from the terminal in Westlake Mall to Seattle Center, the former fair grounds.

Seattle Center is the focal point of the city for conventions, cul-tural programs, and educational displays. An opera house, exhibition hall, and science center are major units in the group. Fascinating ex-hibits depicting scientific progress are housed in the Pacific Science Center, a beautiful structure with lacy white arches and shallow pools where fountains play. From the nearby Space Needle observation deck, six hundred feet up, the city can be viewed in all directions.

Many landmarks of early days in Seattle are gone. Many customs and sights of the era before World War II are just memories. Some years ago Denny Hill was removed and dumped into Elliott Bay. The Indian women no longer sit on the sidewalk of Second Avenue in front of Rhode's Department Store to sell baskets to passersby. The Golden Potlatch, a week of festivities once held to celebrate Seattle's ties with Alaska, has given way to the week-long Seafair with parades, pageants, and a gang of Seafair pirates that take over the town. The old Pike Street Market with its stalls of vegetables, fruit, flowers, and fish, overlooking Elliott Bay is still a cherished part of the life of the city. Most of the houseboats that fringed the shores of Lake Union are gone; however, a few houseboat colonies remain today despite efforts to discourage this type of home. One of the largest colonies is moored along the shore of Portage Bay near the approach to the floating bridge from Evergreen Point.

About fifty years ago a canal was opened to accommodate ocean-going vessels linking salt-water Salmon Bay with fresh-water Lake Washington. At the Salmon Bay end the Ballard Locks lift ships twenty-six feet to the level of Lake Union and across this lake another section of canal permits them to enter Lake Washington. This is the

Lake Washington Ship Canal. For many years a fleet of whaling vessels operating in the North Pacific passed through the canal to their winter moorings in Lake Washington. Canal traffic in recent years, however, has consisted mainly of pleasure craft bound for cruises of the channels and inlets of Puget Sound. This canal has provided Seattle with a fresh-water harbor in addition to its main salt-water harbor in Elliott Bay. Although Elliott Bay is large, little effect is felt there from the winter storms that lash the Washington coast or the entrance to the Strait of Juan de Fuca no more than a hundred miles away. It is a major port for many cargo ships since Seattle, on the Great Circle Route that curves northward across the Pacific, is nearer the coastal cities of the Orient than any other large American port.

During the period of rapid growth in the first half of the century Seattleites gave little thought to building a handsome city. Nature provided a beautiful setting of hills and distant snow-capped mountains,

The Space Needle towers above Seattle Center, the former grounds for the World's Fair of 1962.

inlets, bays and lakes, however, the city itself was a victim of poor city planning. In recent decades steps have been taken to compensate for this neglect. Other than a few small squares, parks with trees are noticeably absent from the central district. A waterfront that could have been developed into one of exceptional beauty is marred by railroad tracks, an unattractive viaduct and heavy truck traffic to wholesale houses and piers. A move to embellish the entrances of many new buildings with attractive fountains and decorative sculptures has made noticeable progress. During Century '21 trees were planted along some of the downtown streets. The fountain sculptures of George Tsutakawa, a professor at the University of Washington, have contributed a touch of real beauty in the heart of the city. One of Tsutakawa's bronze fountain sculptures stands at the Fifth Avenue entrance to Seattle's new main library.

The University of Washington, which began as the Washington Territorial University on a ten-acre tract where the Olympic Hotel stands today, now occupies a large area of land between Lake Union and Lake Washington in the northeastern part of the city. Part of the campus was used for the Alaska-Yukon-Pacific Exposition in 1909 and since then new buildings have been added frequently to accommodate an ever growing student body. Now, with most of its many buildings in the Gothic style of architecture, it has a total enrollment of slightly more than 25,000 students.

Seattle has an urban population of more than 557,000; its metropolitan area has over 1,187,000 people. And thousands more come to live in Seattle and its environs all the time.

Portland grew slowly and sensibly except during World War II when one hundred thousand workers flocked to its shipyards. In the early 1900s dredging of the lower Columbia for a deeper channel and construction of breakwaters at the mouth of the river brought more ocean-going vessels and consequently more commerce to its harbor. Portland became a world port for the shipping of grain from the Columbia River Basin, lumber and wood products from Oregon's forests, and supplies for Alaska.

The city lies on both sides of the Willamette River. The older part, commonly called the West Side, occupies the original site where Indians had carved a niche in the forest for a canoe landing. This is the business district. Expansion farther west is hindered by high cliffs just a few streets back from the river. Streets in the area, like Washington, Alder, and Morrison streets, are narrow. They were limited to one-way traffic long before this method of relieving traffic congestion was

Portland, the largest city in Oregon, lies in the shadow of majestic Mount Hood. The Willamette River, in the foreground, winds through Portland's business district.

adopted by other cities. Elm-shaded parks brightened by hundreds of rosebushes that bloom from May to November lie in the heart of the business section. Portland long has been known as a quiet tree-shaded city which still retains some of the New England atmosphere her pioneer residents brought with them when they came west.

Portland Heights, the residential district on the hill overlooking the downtown area offers views Portlanders like visitors to see. The white cone of Mount Hood looms up in the east and to the northeast are the snow-crested peaks of Mount St. Helens and Mount Adams across the Columbia in Washington. In Washington Park are the International Rose Test Gardens where new varieties of roses from all parts of the world are planted and tested in the western Oregon climate which is ideal for growing roses.

The city's East Side spreads across the valley floor toward the foothills of the Cascade Range. Small manufacturing plants and shops occupy much of this area which parallels the river. Beyond lie residential areas and ample room for future growth. Lloyd Center, one of the most elaborate shopping centers of the west, has an ice-skating rink enclosed by branches of the city's leading stores and balcony restaurants overlooking the rink where one can dine and watch the fun. South along the river are lumber and wood-processing mills. Lumber and wheat have long been the basis of the city's economy. Portland is often called the "Lumber Capital of the World." Since the completion of several northwest dams producing low-cost hydroelectric power, the aluminum plant at Troutdale and several other electrochemical industries have been attracted to the Portland area.

Late in the 1880s Portlanders decided their home town should be the "Rose City" of the nation. The idea originated with Mrs. Henry Pittock. She had a big tent put up in the front yard of her home in what is now downtown Portland. Rose lovers were invited to display their finest roses. This was the city's first rose show. It became an annual event. About 1906 it was decided a week of festivities would be more appropriate and the Portland Rose Festival was born. During the first ten years of the festivals the "Electrical Parade" of illuminated floats on flat cars was the main feature of the celebration. Ever since then, however, at the beginning of June, Portlanders have adorned the streets in the heart of the city with pink and green banners and the emblem of the rose. A queen and a court of princesses are crowned, a parade of flower-bedecked floats moves through the city, and other events are scheduled.

Portland has an urban population of approximately 372,676, and its metropolitan area has about 876,000 people. The urban population is slightly less than that of Louisville, Kentucky.

Up in British Columbia nature has given Vancouver a setting of mountains, inlets, and valleys that helps to compensate for any unattractive areas in this sprawling Canadian city. Burrard Inlet, spanned by the high Lions Gate Bridge at the harbor entrance and the Second Narrows Bridge farther east, is its northern limit. The municipalities of West Vancouver and North Vancouver are spread along the opposite shore on a shelf of land at the base of Hollyburn and Grouse mountains. In back of these are the two Coast Range peaks called The Lions. The north arm of the Fraser River, rimmed with log booms to be towed to the mills, lies to the south. Planes circle over Lulu Island across the river above the runways of Vancouver International Airport.

Aerial view of Vancouver, British Columbia, showing part of Stanley Park at the left and English Bay below with its crescent of white sand beach

This is Canada's only big west coast port. From here wheat from the prairie provinces, minerals from the mountains of British Columbia and Alberta, and lumber and wood products are shipped to all parts of the world. Coastal vessels shuttle between Vancouver and towns of the islands and mainland as far north as Alaska. Barges loaded with sawdust from the mills or freight cars bound for Nanaimo pass under Lions Gate Bridge and into the Strait of Georgia.

Vancouver is a cosmopolitan city. Sailors from ships in port, East Indian women in flowing saris or men wearing turbans, new Canadians in German lederhosen, English couples walking the seven miles around Stanley Park, Italians, and Yugoslavs are all a part of the Vancouver scene. A Chinaman in coolie garb with crates of eggs or farm produce slung from a carrying pole might be seen delivering to markets on

Hastings Street. So many people of Germanic origin come to shop on Robson Street that Vancouverites have dubbed it Robson Strasse. Here are the German *konditorei* where only pastry and coffee are served, stores brimming with English bone china, German toys, Norwegian imports, textiles and brassware from India, and sausage shops. In the heart of the thoroughfare is Murchie's where a customer can purchase any blend of coffee or brand of tea.

Next to the mountains of the North Shore and the sea, Vancouver's greatest recreational asset is Stanley Park which is within walking distance of the heart of the retail district. It is a thousand-acre peninsula between Burrard Inlet and English Bay with a forest of giant trees and the secluded wilderness of Beaver Lake. Wild ducks and swans nest among the reeds and in midsummer the whole lake becomes a garden where thousands of waterlilies bloom. Youngsters enjoy the children's zoo and the finest aquarium on the Pacific Coast where a killer whale, dolphins, and all the fantastic undersea life of the Strait of Georgia are on display. According to a long-standing custom the nine o'clock gun booms each evening from Brockton Point on the park drive.

Vancouverites are a people of varied interests. On winter weekends the ski runs on Mount Seymour and Grouse Mountain, just a few minutes' drive from the heart of the city, are popular spots. Chinatown on Pender Street with its Oriental shops and cafés draws evening visitors as does the new Queen Elizabeth Theater. The city has two fine universities, the new Simon Fraser atop a hill overlooking the harbor, and the University of British Columbia above Spanish Banks overlooking the Strait of Georgia.

Except for the sawmills along the Fraser River and Burrard Inlet, the oil refineries, and Vancouver's busy port there are not many large industrial facilities within the city. Vancouver is the big trading and distributing center for the province. In winter, when heavy snows in the mountains halt logging operations, loggers flock to the city. This influx often contributes to the winter increase in the number of unemployed. Vancouver has an urban population of more than four hundred thousand. There are between eight and nine hundred thousand in the metropolitan area.

Industry in the Pacific Northwest

FUR, FORESTS, AND FISH built the first industries of the Pacific Northwest. They were the wealth of the canoe people. When traders came sea otters and beaver were slaughtered to satisfy their lust for furs. The fur brigades of the trading companies trapped with no thought of the future. As a result of their excesses, the fur industry died in the region slightly more than a century ago. Then settlers came to live in the valleys. When they arrived, forests reached to the timberline of high mountain ranges and covered the land to the edge of the sea. Trees had to be cut to make room for cabins and niches were carved out of the forest so that wheat and potatoes could be grown. When the first sawmill was built at Oregon City in 1842 trees were cut down in quantity for lumber.

Salmon choked most of the streams of the northwest in summers before there were many towns and the Indians would reap vast harvests with nets and traps. Settlers soon adopted their fruitful methods of fishing. They salted the catch in barrels and sent it aboard sailing ships to markets on the Atlantic seaboard. In 1866 the first cannery in the region was built on the Columbia. Ships from Boston came up the Columbia and into the Willamette to load lumber and salted and pickled salmon. Small towns on the shores of Puget Sound became lumber ports from which cargoes of timber were sent across the Pacific to the Orient.

Forests were depleted in the east and the Great Lakes region of the middle west at the beginning of this century as a result of wasteful logging methods. The woodsman's ax and the lumberjack's saw over-harvested crops that nature had toiled forty to eighty years to produce. Logged-off land was burned since none were aware at that time that the burning also destroyed the seeds and seedlings that could have started another crop of trees. When these forests were gone timber barons looked toward the Pacific Northwest as a source of lumber. They moved in with donkey engines and logging crews. They built bunk-houses and cookhouses. In the dry months of summer their careless-ness started fires, smoke masked the mountains, and thousands of acres of valuable timber were lost. Then the public became concerned.

Some large timber companies also became concerned. The policy of cutting the trees irresponsibly and moving on was wrong. Without forests there would be no trees to cut for the future, and there would be a serious depletion of the wildlife that make the forests their home.

Millions of hardy seedlings are grown on Weyerhaeuser Timber Company tree nurseries. The seedlings are then transplanted by field crews under the supervision of company foresters.

Forest area selection is used in logging operations today. Selected blocks of timber are cut and intermittent islands of trees are left unharvested to serve as a seed source.

Erosion would be severe and the area's natural beauty would be lost. The public grew resentful and demanded legislation. A few timber companies could see the dim outlook for forest industries if nothing was done. In 1939 the Weyerhaeuser Timber Company set aside more than one hundred thousand acres of land in the Grays Harbor area of western Washington and started a tree farm to remedy the situation. Tree farms and forest nurseries are now located in several parts of the Pacific Northwest.

Conservationists worked during the years when Theodore Roosevelt was president to halt this wanton destruction of a national resource. Roosevelt appointed Gifford Pinchot chief forester of the United States. National forests were expanded and laws enacted to control logging on public lands. Forest management was carried out on a scientific basis. Overcutting was avoided. Two or three trees were planted for every one cut. Timber was harvested in patches or strips so that seeds from the uncut forest would be carried into the logged-off areas to start a new growth for another harvest forty, sixty, or eighty years later. This is known as forest management for sustained yield. Seeding is done by machines or from the air by helicopter. Seedlings from tree nurseries are also planted. In mid-April 1966, one large Canadian timber company planted a two-year-old Douglas fir seedling in the Ash River valley of Vancouver Island, its fifty millionth tree in its reforestation program. Company officials estimate that in eighty years it will stand one hundred feet tall, be more than one and a quarter feet in diameter at a point midway between the top and the base, and yield forty-eight cubic feet of usable wood.

Man's increased scientific knowledge has made timber more important to him today than it was to the timber barons who mowed down whole forests. Wood previously burned through ignorance is now used in the production of pulp and paper. The production of some plastics is based upon the use of cellulose from wood. Logs are cut by a circular peeling of the wood to produce thin layers which are then used in making plywood. More than fifty per cent of the income of Oregon comes from the timber industry. Income from this source is almost as high in Washington, Idaho, and British Columbia.

Fish have always been important to the Pacific Northwest economy. When trading posts were established by the Hudson's Bay and the North West companies, salmon—dried, salted, or smoked—constituted a major food item at each post. Some trading posts along the upper Columbia used as much as twenty-five thousand pounds of salmon a year. It was brought to the posts by canoe brigades. By the end of the nineteenth century a large amount of salmon was being canned. The sockeye-salmon run in the Fraser River in 1901 was one of the greatest in the history of British Columbia and yielded a pack of about one and a quarter million cases of canned fish. Fishing was intensified along the British Columbia coast for other fish as well as salmon. Although the province is only eight hundred miles long, the total coastline measures more than seven thousand miles, if the shores of islands are included with those of the mainland and its inlets. Many fishing villages are spread all along the shores of British Columbia.

The several species of Pacific salmon have a life-history which is different from that of halibut, sole, or other commercially valuable fish. There are five marketable species—sockeye, pink, chum, spring or chinook, and silver salmon. The eggs are deposited in the sand and gravel along the shallow margins near the headwaters of many northwest streams. After hatching, the young fish remain in fresh water for a brief time until they are strong enough to travel down the river to the ocean. After two, five, or more years, depending upon the species, the mature fish leave the ocean to return to the shallow gravel fresh-water beds where they were hatched. There they deposit and fertilize their own eggs. Then, since they are no longer able to live in fresh water, they die after spawning.

When settlers became aware of the demand for canned salmon many ways were devised to catch the fish at the time they began their migrations upstream to spawn. In some areas the entrances to salmon streams were so completely blocked by nets that few fish could avoid being caught. This meant a sharp decrease in the salmon runs two to five years later. Controls were needed and some methods of fishing had to be eliminated. Fishwheels, upright wheels with nets used to lift up quantities of fish from the water and deposit them in scows, were outlawed and fishing seasons and quotas were established. These con-

The grain industry is an important one in the Pacific Northwest. Here shocks of grain lie ready at harvest time in Oregon's Hood River valley.

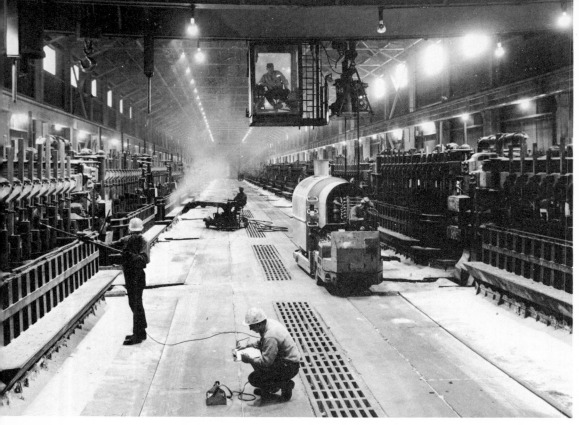

The aluminum smelter at Kitimat, British Columbia. In the foreground, metallurgical technicians check the voltages of each rod carrying electrical energy into the smelting pots. The truck at the right adds alumina to the pots. The machine in the background is used to break the rock-like crust which forms on the surface of the smelting pots.

trols saved the fishing industry from the disaster suffered by the fur industry years before. Where fish in their migrations passed through territorial waters of both the United States and Canada, treaties were made and international commissions given the power to control the fishing. The same was done to protect the halibut fisheries of the North Pacific.

Other industries have come to the Pacific Northwest besides the production of timber, fish, grain, and fruit. The mining industry and the extraction of metals from their ores is of major importance in some parts of the Pacific Northwest. After the feverish search for gold in the nineteenth century had subsided, attention was turned to other metals and rich deposits were found. The metallurgical industries involved in extraction of the metals have flourished, particularly in the Idaho panhandle and in the region around Trail and Nelson in southeastern British Columbia. The availability of low-cost hydroelectric power has made possible the building of installations for the extraction of metals by the use of electricity. Idaho has long been the leading silver-producing state of the nation. Smelters in the Idaho panhandle also extract other metals from the ores which contain the silver, such as lead and zinc. Some gold is also found. Silver, lead, and zinc ingots are the principal products of the big smelter at Trail in southeastern British Columbia. Copper is mined along the British Columbia coast at Brittania. Industrial minerals, of which there are many deposits in the Pacific Northwest, include diatomaceous earth, vermiculite, and phosphate rock. The diatomaceous earth is needed for filters in several industries such as food-processing, paper production, and the manufacture of plastics. Vermiculite, consisting largely of flakes of mica, is an insulating material. Commercial fertilizers are made from phosphate rock.

Industries which use the produce of northwest farms and ranches are of major importance. Sugar refineries process the huge quantities of sugar beets grown in Idaho, eastern Washington, and some parts of Oregon. The production of potato starch is centered in the southern part of Idaho, famous for its potato crops. A number of industries producing meat products and hides are dependent upon the raising of beef cattle.

There are many paper and pulp mills in the region west of the Cascade Mountains. Wood from the forests which is not suitable for lumber is utilized in this major northwest industry. One of the largest mills is located at Port Angeles in Washington, another is at Ocean Falls on the British Columbia coast, and still another big mill has been built in Springfield in Oregon's Willamette valley. Much of the wood pulp produced in these mills is shipped east to the paper manufacturers of the northeastern states.

Recreation in the Pacific Northwest

THE OUT-OF-DOORS has an important role in the life of the northwesterner. It is easy to forget the noise and confinement of the city on a hike in high country above the clouds with magnificent panoramas of dazzling blue lakes, green forests, and glistening white peaks. Some families, on any weekend of the year, scramble aboard their cabin cruiser to explore channels, inlets, and bays in a world apart from the routine of everyday living. The rock hounds of the region, of which there are many, trek to mountain streams, desert canyons, or the gravel beds of ocean beaches in search of treasures in garnet, jasper, agate, and petrified wood. In summer and early autumn nature lovers delight in alpine meadows ablaze with great swatches of color. There are flowering shrubs and lush green vegetation in the forests and lakeshore marshes where water fowl nest and red-winged blackbirds cling to cattail stalks while searching for seeds. Deer, elk, bighorn sheep, mountain goats, and beaver attract others to wildlife sanctuaries of the wilderness areas and national forests. Many northwesterners are ardent beachcombers whose happiest hours are spent enjoying the rhythm of roaring breakers and whimpering sea gulls in fog or sunshine. For many more camping in a forest is a pleasure that is as frequent as weekends from May to November. Nature has been lavish in the Pacific Northwest, and people of the region have made the enjoyment of outdoor activities an important part of their life.

Hikers, trail-riders, and campers find the opportunity to see wildlife in its natural haunts. Motorists are frequently thrilled by the sight of big-game animals along mountain highways. And in the national parks and forests where large stands of fir or pine are broken by alpine meadows or lakes rimmed by marshes, these animals are even more plentiful. Dense forests where sunlight seldom reaches the forest floor do not permit the growth of shrubs and grasses upon which they feed. The pine forests of the eastern slopes of the Cascades with their wide open spaces provide an ideal environment for big-game animals.

Deer, moose, and elk inhabit most of the mountain ranges. In winter they move to lower levels in search of food. The mule deer is the common species found in the interior while the blacktail deer makes the Coast Range and Vancouver Island his home. Logged-off land is a favorite grazing ground for these animals. Hunting for deer is permitted during open season in October or November with very definite restrictions. In British Columbia alone sixty thousand deer are taken annually by resident hunters. Moose are less abundant. They frequent the marshes and grasslands which lie between mountain ranges. Moose like to wade among the reeds along the margins of lakes in search of succulent roots and sprouts. Herds of elk roam through the wilderness of the mountainous regions of Idaho, throughout the Cascade Range, and in the East Kootenay district of southern British Columbia. Mountain caribou, which are the reindeer of North America, inhabit the virgin forests of remote areas of British Columbia, particularly the Monashee Mountains. Since these animals feed principally on lichens growing on the bark of tree trunks and branches they are found in forests of old trees rather than in forests of second growth timber.

Bighorn sheep and mountain goats always attract attention. Their natural habitat in this region is the rocky slopes of the Cascades and the ranges of the Rockies. Mountain goats, shy and sure-footed, also range over the rocky ridges and crags of Olympic National Park.

The black bear is the most common northwest species. It lives in the forests of the mountain ranges and sometimes roams into sparsely settled localities where it becomes a nuisance. Berries, fish, and wild honey are its favorite foods. Far to the north in British Columbia, away from towns and logging camps, there are grizzly bears. These are larger, more powerful animals. When cruising along the "Inside Passage" one can often see grizzlies at the water's edge or on partially submerged driftwood trying to scoop up an unwary salmon. Raccoons, smallest members of the bear family, are plentiful. They rear their young in hollow trees in the forests of relatively moist regions. The beaver, almost exterminated in some areas by the fur brigades of a

Elk are often seen in the mountainous regions of the Pacific Northwest.

hundred and fifty years ago, inhabits many parts of the intermountain region today. Its home of mud and sticks built in a pond formed by its own dam is always an interesting sight. Campers in desert country south of Boise or the forests or sagebrush country of central Oregon and Washington grow accustomed to the howl of the coyote that breaks the quiet of the night. Timber wolves, bobcats, and cougars also live in the remote forests.

Bird watchers will find few regions that surpass the Pacific Northwest in the variety and abundance of birds to be seen there. A great many species are found in the woods and forests. Migratory waterfowl use the lakes of intermountain regions for a rest stop or nesting area during their travels over the continent. Lakes in southern Oregon and in the Okanogan country, and many in southern Idaho swarm with various species of ducks and geese in summer and autumn. Flocks of gulls, terns, curlews, grebes, and other shore birds can be seen when beachcombing or fishing in coastal waters. Ring-neck pheasants inhabit the plains and meadows and nest where food is plentiful in the fields of grain. There are several species of grouse, hawks, woodpeckers, and jays. Campers quickly learn about the gray jay's skill in clearing an unwatched picnic table of lunch and stealing food from any tent in which it is stored. These bold birds congregate around the picnic areas of most of the national parks. They are commonly called "camp robbers."

An extensive network of well-marked trails leads through unspoiled mountain country and wilderness areas of the interior and along the Oregon and Washington coasts. Some at high altitudes are recommended for experienced hikers only. Although these are well maintained by rangers of the United States Forest Service they do include some stretches of difficult terrain in the vicinity of some of the highest peaks. The Cascade Crest Trail threads its way along the hump of the Cascade Range from the Canadian border to the Columbia River entirely within the borders of national forests. Oregon's Skyline Trail takes up where the Cascade Crest Trail leaves off and extends to the California state line. There are also hundreds of shorter trails to be enjoyed in the Pacific Northwest like those in Manning Park in the Cascades just across the Canadian border.

Mount Rainier Park is very popular with hikers. Its ninety-mile Wonderland Trail encircles the big snow-capped peak. Another trail offers a seven-mile round-trip hike from Tahoma Creek Campground to Indian Henry's Hunting Ground. Shorter trails begin in Yakima Park which is reached by the highway over Chinook Pass. They lead to alpine flower fields, lakes, and spectacular views of the big snow-capped peak. Experienced mountaineers find the climb up the glacier-mantled slopes of Mount Rainier a challenge to their skill. Mount Hood in Oregon is also encircled by a trail. This is the thirty-six-mile Timberline Trail. Dozens of other interesting hikes can be made near Mount Hood from shorter trails that radiate from Timberline Lodge near the base of the mountain.

In recent years the Mount Adams Wilderness Area in southern Washington has become a favorite of hikers. Since it is off the beaten tourist track and quite isolated from the crowds of summer visitors its large well-planned campground is quiet and desirable. The campsites are located in a forest of pines mixed with firs. This area is most easily reached by a Forest Service road from Trout Lake to Bird Creek Meadows. From here one trail leads to the south side of the peak which is covered with snow and where winter fun can be enjoyed in midsummer. The summit can be climbed in about five or six hours from the end of this trail. In autumn a spectacular display of color comes to the slopes around the campground at Bird Creek Meadows when the leaves of the wild huckleberry bushes turn golden yellow.

Each of the three Pacific Northwest states has between three and four hundred campgrounds, some with as many as four hundred camp-sites and trailer spaces. All are located in scenic spots and many provide sturdy picnic tables. Some have outdoor fireplaces and community kitchens. Although British Columbia has no areas which correspond exactly to our national forests, similar facilities are provided in the provincial parks in many parts of the southern half of the province.

A number of attractive Forest Service camps are situated along the picturesque Nooksack River between Mount Shuksan and Mount Baker not many miles from Bellingham in northwestern Washington. From these some well-marked trails lead to both of the snow-capped

View of Deception Pass from the Deception Pass State Park in Washington

peaks, passing some beautiful alpine lakes and mountain streams along the way. Distinctly different is the camping area of Deception Pass State Park which extends into both Fidalgo and Whidbey Islands on either side of the narrow channel between these two islands located below the San Juan Islands in Puget Sound. This is one of Washington's most popular state parks. Pleasure craft can be moored at the park's docks, clams can be dug on the beaches, and made into steaming bowls of chowder right on the spot in its outdoor kitchens. Beachcombers can find bits of driftwood, shells, starfish, and tide pools well-populated with fantastic seashore creatures at ebb tide. Another delightful Forest Service campground is in the Blue Mountain Recreation Area of southeastern Washington not far from Walla Walla. There are also many privately operated dude or guest ranches in the Blue Mountains. Sun Lakes State Park on the floor of the Grand Coulee at the foot of Dry Falls in central Washington offers a semidesert environment for guests in its campground within a short driving distance from Soap Lake and Grand Coulee Dam. Lake Chelan lies in a deep, narrow basin gouged out by prehistoric glaciers on the edge of the North Cascades region of eastern Washington. Here, nine miles from the town of Chelan in Lake Chelan State Park, are public campgrounds that provide both camp and trailer sites, an ideal vacation spot for those who enjoy swimming, boating, and hiking. Mount St. Helens, its snow-covered symmetrical cone mirrored in big Spirit Lake in south-central Washington, is the major attraction of the Forest Service public campground in the forest along the lake shore. Trails lead from it to many parts of the area where elk graze and black bear gorge themselves on huckleberries in late summer. A number of popular public camping areas, all of which provide space for trailers, are located on the shores of some of the man-made lakes formed by dams built in the Columbia Basin. Big Moran State Park on Orcas Island in the San Juan archipelago of Puget Sound, Sequim Bay State Park which is near historic Port Townsend in the sunniest part of western Washington, and the Forest Service campground at the end of the road that parallels the Hoh River in the rain forest area of Olympic National Park are also unusually attractive.

Equally well developed are Oregon's facilities for those who love the out-of-doors. This state has one of the finest systems of wayside picnic areas in the entire northwest. Especially attractive are those areas along the Oregon Coast Highway, in the passes of the Cascades, in the Willamette valley, and in Rogue River country. Close to forty state parks have been established within sight of the Pacific Ocean and they are supplemented by recreation areas under the control of the

Anthony Lakes at the foot of Gunsight Mountain is a popular recreation area in eastern Oregon.

Forest Service. An outstanding example is the Jessie M. Honeymoon State Park with over three hundred camp or trailer sites beside two small fresh-water lakes and almost within a stone's throw of the ocean. Stone fireplaces, picnic tables, and trails that wind up the slopes of Heceta Head for breath-taking views of the coast are provided. Devil's Elbow State Park and the Umpqua Lighthouse State Park have excellent picnic areas. There are Forest Service camps to accommodate hundreds of vacationers in the Cascades along the North Umpqua River east of Roseburg. In the wilderness surrounding the Three Sisters, the Lake of the Woods Recreation Area northwest of Klamath Falls has campsites and a couple of hundred miles of trails. At some of the campgrounds saddle or pack horses can be rented for trips into areas of great natural beauty inhabited by mule deer and black bear. Most of the public campgrounds east of the crest of the Cascades are in forest or lake country. This is true of the Blue and the Wallowa mountain areas, the home of bighorn sheep. Others are in the forests and canyons of the country along the course of the John Day, Crooked, and Deschutes rivers.

Idaho has its share of national forests. Samowen Campground in Kaniksu National Forest is on the east shore of Lake Pend Oreille with sites for camps, trailers, and boat launchings. Idaho's lakes and climate in which summer nights are cool contribute to the fun of camping there. Campsites along the Salmon River in Challis National Forest and Redfish Lake Forest Camp, one of the largest in Idaho, are in beautiful wilderness areas. At Alturas Lake Forest Camp, not far from Sun Valley and in the Sawtooth Mountains, campers can enjoy horseback riding, guided nature walks, and lectures by rangers around the campfire in the evening.

There are many camps in both provincial and national parks in British Columbia, most of them in the lower half of the province from the Fraser valley to the foothills of the Rockies. A few miles north of Vancouver on what is called the "Sunshine Coast," Alice Lake Park has more than eighty units and picnic tables. The Barkerville Historic Park, where the gold-rush boom-town of Barkerville has been reconstructed as a centennial project, has three public campgrounds. Little more than fifty miles east of Vancouver the camping areas of Cultus Lake Provincial Park in the Fraser valley have more than three hundred campsites. Goldstream Park near Malahat Mountain on Vancouver Island, a few miles west of Victoria, has campsites and picnic tables. One of the finest is Manning Provincial Park on the Trans-Canada Highway between Hope and Penticton with five public camping areas. Bears frequent the garbage dump only a couple of miles from the lodge. Trails lead to many forest vantage points. Okanagan Lake Park near Kelowna has sites for campers on terraces overlooking the lake in a region which is semidesert. The Shuswap Lake Park east of Kamloops is especially attractive in autumn when the leaves of the hardwood trees turn red and yellow and sockeye salmon migrate to their spawning grounds in nearby Adams River. Nearly two hundred and fifty provincial parks have been established in British Columbia. Some are very small and without campsites and are managed by local park boards. The largest is Tweedsmuir Provincial Park covering 2,424,400 acres. There are four national parks in British Columbia— Glacier, Kootenay, Mount Revelstoke, and Yoho. All but Mount Revelstoke National Park have excellent campgrounds.

Dude or guest ranches are a traditional institution in the west and there are many of them in the Pacific Northwest. They are usually large ranches where herds of beef cattle are raised. Guests pay a weekly or monthly rate for their stay there. Some of the largest ranches offer many different ways of whiling away the hours such as horseback riding, an opportunity to join ranch hands or cowboys in their routine chores, hikes, and evening dances and social activities of various kinds. There are guest ranches in the vicinity of Yakima, Ellensburg, and Wenatchee in Washington and near Bend and Klamath Falls, in central Oregon. Many dude ranches are located along the western edge of the Idaho panhandle, in parts of the Snake River valley and the foothills of the Sawtooth Mountains. The Okanagan Lake country and the Chilcotin and Cariboo districts of British Columbia are the principal areas of the province with guest ranches.

An enormous increase has occurred in the last couple of decades in the number of small-boat and yacht owners in the cities of the coast and Puget Sound regions of the Pacific Northwest. Seattle boasts of being the "small-boat capital of the nation." The number of marinas in the city and the great exodus of motorists with boat-carrying trailers each weekend tends to prove this claim. Many a home in Seattle's residential districts has a boat parked in or beside the garage. Across the border in Vancouver, in the small towns of the southern mainland, and on Vancouver Island the quota of boating enthusiasts is also high. On sunny days small boats with red, white, or blue sails move out into the water of Vancouver's English Bay toward the coves and channels along the North Shore. Boating is also popular on the lakes of central Washington and on Pend Oreille, Priest, and Payette lakes in Idaho. Regattas are held on some of the region's largest lakes during the summer. Puget Sound, with its protected waters, vast network of channels, and its hundreds of islands, is an ideal area for this type of recreation. For those who do not own or rent a boat the state of Washington ferry system links Seattle, Tacoma, and other large cities with the islands and distant peninsulas of this inland water playground.

Skiing is the popular winter sport of the region. There are a large number of ski areas throughout the Pacific Northwest, some of them known internationally, where skiers flock on weekends or for a week or two of winter fun. Snow conditions are usually good starting about the first of December and lasting until the end of March. Whistler Mountain, a newly developed ski resort in the mountains north of Vancouver, British Columbia, has skiing as late as early July. Snoqualmie Pass in the Cascades east of Seattle is Washington's most popular winter fun center where visitors enjoy skiing, tobogganing, sledding and, on some evenings, skiing under floodlights. The ski areas at Mount Baker, Mount Rainier National Park, Stevens Pass, Blewett Pass, White Pass, and Mount Spokane are also popular. Portlanders enjoy the ski areas

Skiing at Sun Valley, Idaho

at Government Camp and Timberline Lodge near Mount Hood. Other Oregon winter sports areas are located at Crater Lake, Hoodoo Bowl in the Santiam Pass region, La Grande, and Bend. The most famous ski resort in Idaho is Sun Valley. One of the finest in British Columbia is Tod Mountain near Kamloops where the dry air of the interior provides fine powder snow during most of the season. Vancouverites have three ski areas just outside the borders of the city—Grouse Mountain, Hollyburn, and Mount Seymour. In the Snoqualmie, Mount Baker, and Mount Hood areas several slalom ski races and ski tournaments are held during the winter months.

Thousands of northwesterners make frequent fishing trips to the region's sounds, bays, and coastal waters. Those who fish the streams and lakes beyond the Cascades and Coast Range find them well stocked with fish reared in state and provincial hatcheries. During the smelt runs when thousands of these small fish crowd the streams of southwestern Washington fishermen swarm out from the riverbanks in small boats with dip nets and pails to get a share of the harvest. Salmon derbies are major events for amateur fishermen in the salt-water areas. A salmon derby is a contest in which automobiles or other valuable prizes are offered to those who have qualified in preliminary contests. The winners are the fishermen who catch the largest salmon within certain specified time limits. Observers accompany contestants to see that the rules of the derby are scrupulously followed. Derby Day occurs at the time salmon enter the Strait of Juan de Fuca, the Gulf of Georgia, Puget Sound, or the estuaries of some of the rivers to begin their migration to the spawning grounds near the headwaters of northwest streams. This occurs in late August or early September. Derbies are held off Port Townsend and Port Angeles along the strait, in Puget Sound, near West Vancouver in British Columbia, and at Ilwaco and Westport on the Washington coast. A big fish, a big prize, and the envy of fellow contestants is the winner's reward.

Puget Sound and the island and coastal beaches reveal a fascinating world of seashore life at ebb tide. It is this realm of strange marine animals and plants that tempts beachcombers to explore. Quite often a whale that has ventured too close to shore is stranded on the beach. Animals usually found range from big starfish of red, purple, or orange hue to tiny limpets which cling by the thousands to rocks. There are giant kelp and delicate feathery varieties of marine algae strewn about. Disk-like sand dollars are unusually abundant after a storm. Along the coast spherical glass floats released from the nets of Japanese fishermen drift ashore after being carried across the Pacific by ocean currents. These are just a few of the mementoes that make trudging over drifting sand and tangled driftwood a pleasure.

A carefree day spent in a picturesque fishing village in Puget Sound or on one of the islands farther north can mean many happy hours for the patient observer. From the edge of a dock or a rowboat offshore marine life can be seen in a leisurely way. Brightly colored starfish, gorgeous clusters of flowerlike sea anemones, brilliant orange sea carrots and many other forms of marine life that look more like plants than animals cling to barnacle-encrusted piling. Small transparent jellyfish and whole schools of spindly candlefish catch the eye.

Other northwesterners find pleasure in colorful annual events, or in visiting the region's many historical places and museums. Idaho, Oregon, and British Columbia have an excellent program for providing markers along the highways to designate historic sites and other points of interest. Rambling through a lonely ghost town or a beachside Indian village along the coast can make history vivid and meaningful.

Festivals are red-letter days on Pacific Northwest calendars. Such major events as Portland's Rose Festival and Wenatchee's Apple Blossom Festival are especially well-known. May brings rhododendron festivals to Port Townsend, Washington, and Florence, Oregon, as well as Spokane's famous Lilac Festival and the Azalea Festival at Brook-

The rugged coastline of the Pacific Northwest is a beachcomber's paradise. Tide pools such as these along the Oregon coast reveal a fantastic variety of seashore life.

ings, Oregon. In April the queen of the Puyallup Valley Daffodil Festival and her princesses ride flower-bedecked floats in a parade down the main streets of Tacoma, Sumner, and Puyallup. From midsummer to late autumn cowboys rope steers, ride bucking broncos, and join in chuck-wagon dinners served during the dozens of rodeos and stampedes held in most of the region from the crest of the Cascades to the foothills of the Rockies. Idaho Falls, Coulee City, Ellensburg, Eugene, and Burns go ultra-western and Indians and visitors congregate to enjoy the fun. The climax of the rodeo and roundup season is the great western classic, the Pendleton Roundup, in mid-September. Celebrations that revive traditional Indian rites and customs attended by tribal members in full regalia are held in the Yakima valley and at Klamath Falls. As harvest time approaches and on through September and October, county and state fairs are held. The Oregon State Fair in Salem has long been one of the finest.

Historically the Pacific Northwest is young and yet it is rich in its cultural heritage. Indian customs and crafts once flourished throughout the region, and northwesterners today find pleasure in touring those areas where some vestiges of early Indian ways remain. In the Hazelton district of British Columbia totem poles made from cedar by ancient carvers still stand. The newly constructed Haida village in Vancouver, the Indian canoe races on Puget Sound near Coupeville and extensive collections of Indian arts and crafts in museums in Seattle, Tacoma, Boise, Vancouver, and Victoria are all interesting places to visit. Reconstructions and sites such as Cataldo Mission on the Coeur d'Alene River, Fort Clatsop near Astoria, and Fort Nisqually in Tacoma's Point Defiance Park help visitors to picture events during the period of settlement. Relics of early times are housed in the Museum of History and Industry in Seattle and the Museum of Science and Industry in Portland. The Logging Museum in Tacoma and the State Historical Society Museum in Julia Davis Park in Boise have interesting regional displays. Seattle's art museum in Volunteer Park attracts many visitors because of its highly rated collection of Oriental and Islamic art.

The Pacific Northwest is an attractive vacation land for those who seek a region which provides a great variety of recreational opportunities in an ideal environment. The summers there are sunny and generally unmarred by rainy days. Sunlight filters through the region's forests and enhances the beauty of its mountain streams, snow-capped peaks, and rugged coasts. The Pacific Northwest is many things to many people. A vacation spent there can be a fascinating, happy experience.

Index